# The Subversive Role of Visions in Early Christian Martyrs

Zaida Maldonado Pérez

*Asbury Theological Seminary Series in
World Christian Revitalization Movements in Early Church Studies, No. 1*

EMETH PRESS
www.emethpress.com

The Subversive Role of Visions in Early Christian Martyrs

Copyright © 2011  Zaida Maldonado Pérez
Printed in the United States of America on acid-free paper

All rights reserved. No part of this book may be reproduced, or stored in a retrieval system or transmitted in any form or by any means, electronic, mechanical, photocopying, recording, scanning or otherwise, except as permitted by the 1976 United States Copyright Act, or with the prior written permission of Emeth Press. Requests for permission should be addressed to: Emeth Press, P. O. Box 23961, Lexington, KY 40523-3961.   http://www.emethpress.com.

Library of Congress Cataloging-in-Publication Data

Maldonado Pérez, Zaida, 1957-
  The subversive role of visions in early Christian martyrs / Zaida Maldonado Pérez.
    p. cm. -- (Asbury Theological Seminary series in world Christian revitalization movements in early church studies ; no. 1)
  Includes bibliographical references (p.     ) and index.
  ISBN 978-1-60947-011-1 (alk. paper)
  1. Martyrologies--History and criticism. 2. Visions--History of doctrines--Early church, ca. 30-600. I. Title.
  BR1609.M36 2011
  272'.1--dc22                                                           2010033508


Front Cover
A copy on the front cover of the art by Jean-Léon Gérôme (1824–1904) is known as "The Christian Martyrs' Last Prayer." Public Domain.

# The Asbury Theological Seminary Series in Christian Revitalization Studies

This volume is published in collaboration with the Center for the Study of World Christian Revitalization Movements, a cooperative initiative of Asbury Theological Seminary faculty. Building on the work of the previous Wesleyan/Holiness Studies Center at the Seminary, the Center provides a focus for research in the Wesleyan Holiness and other related Christian renewal movements, including Pietism and Pentecostal movements, which have had a world impact. The research seeks to develop analytical models of these movements, including their biblical and theological assessment. Using an interdisciplinary approach, the Center bridges relevant discourses in several areas in order to gain insights for effective Christian mission globally. It recognizes the need for conducting research that combines insights from the history of evangelical renewal and revival movements with anthropological and religious studies literature on revitalization movements. It also networks with similar or related research and study centers around the world, in addition to sponsoring its own research projects.

Professor Zaida Perez' study of the "subversive role" of visions in early Christian martyrs opens new ground in revitalization research by investigating dreams and visions as prophetic, theocentric imagery and as marks of authenticity in the literature of Christian revitalization movements, past and present. And so it is fitting that her study of visions in the literature of the early Christian martyrs be presented here as the first title published in the Early Church section of this series. The interpretation of their visions, as she demonstrates, provides important insight into the emerging theological understanding of early Christian laity, that stood in defiance of the often oppressive pre-Christian religious systems of classical antiquity.

J. Steven O'Malley
Director, Center for the Study of World
Christian Revitalization Movements and
General Editor, The Asbury Theological
Seminary Series in Christian Revitalization
Studies

# Sub-Series Foreword
# Early and Patristic Christian Studies

In the context of the persecuted church before the Edict of Milan (313 CE) that granted religious freedom to Christians, the emperors of the Greco-Roman states had special purpose in using torture (suffering and the threat of death) to persecute and threaten Christians. However, the book reveals strikingly the other dimension—the subversive dimension of persecution and martyrdom, particularly the role of visions of the martyrs in early Christianity. By death and martyrdom, these Christians subverted the goals and purposes of the principalities of this world and encouraged the Christian communities and affirmed the promised glory awaiting them after death. The end of their lives is but "the day of salvation." Death is subverted by new life, power by powerlessness, and the world by the triumph of Christ's death and resurrection in which the martyr participates (Imitatio Christi).

Using Cyprian's definition of martyr and Karl Rahner's criteria of freedom, the author Zaida Perez defines the term "martyr" as "those Christians of the second to fourth centuries who, given the choice between confessing Christ and apostatizing, willingly chose to confess Christ, underwent suffering, and consummated their confession through their death or proximate death" (5). Perez's carefully defined and interpreted study explores (with the questions she raises beyond Garcia-Rivera's method) the martyrs' visions as prophetic and as communal property and the early church's use of the Acts of the Martyrs as a subversive force against the church's oppressors. In so doing, *The Subversive Role of Visions in Early Christian Martyrs* not only demonstrates the significance and popularity of the visions of the martyrological hagiographical literature of the second to early fourth centuries in their own socio-cultural political context (mainly through historical theological approach), but also gives us a critical contribution and a relevant guide in understanding the role of visions in the suffering Christian communities of the recent world Christian revitalization movements, especially among "Southern Christianity" (by Philip Jenkins) or "Majority World Christianity" (by Lausanne Committee of World Evangelical Fellowship).

Meesaeng Lee Choi, Ph.D.
Editor for the Sub-series on Early and Patristic Christian Studies

# DEDICATION

My Children, Alexander Luis and Jazzlin Ruth,

My Husband, Luis,

My Parents, Ruth and Alfredo Maldonado

You all are such a blessing in my life!

# Contents

Chapter 1. Introduction ................................................................1

Chapter 2. The Visions of the Martyrs and the Role of Subversion...............13

Chapter 3. Visions and the Acts of the Martyrs......................................21

Chapter. 4. Death and the "Hour of Triumph": Subversion within the
    Visions of Saturus and Polycarp..........................................31

Chapter 5. An Exegesis and Biblical Intertextuality of the
    Vision of Saturus...............................................................43

Chapter 6. Mediator, Leader and Advocate: Perpetua's Ministerial
    Role Considered...............................................................77

Concluding Essay......................................................................91

Appendix A..............................................................................93

Appendix B..............................................................................95

Bibliography............................................................................99

# Chapter 1

# Introduction

O sleep more intense than all our waking hours! How happily he sleeps this sleep who is awake by faith! For that sleep had dulled merely his earthly members, for only his spirit could see the Lord. How joyful, how uplifted must we believe the souls of the martyrs were when just as they were on the point of suffering for the confession of the holy Name, they were permitted to hear and see Christ beforehand, offering himself for his dear ones at every place and every time. The restless jolting of the moving carriage was no obstacle, nor even the midday that blazed under a brilliant sun. He does not wait for the solitude of night; by a new kind of grace the Lord has chosen for his martyr a new time for revelation.[1]

The term *vision* is a protean term that has been defined by psychology and religion in a myriad of ways. In religion it has been broadly defined as a visual imagery believed to be "supernatural in origin and revelatory in significance."[2] Visions have further been classified by their forms—normal dreams, vivid memories, vigorous imaginings, and so forth.[3] The early church, however, did not concern itself with these distinctions; rather, it focused on the role and significance of the content of the visions for people's daily lives. This study will assume that perspective and concentrate on what we can learn from the *role* and *content* of the visions of the martyrs about the emerging church and its times. Broadly stated, it is the premise of this book that when considered within their particular historical and theological contexts, the visions of the martyrs can provide important insights into the church of the second to early fourth centuries.

For instance, we know that the martyrological hagiographical literature of the second to early fourth centuries became popular reading and devotional material.[4] Why? And, what role did the visions themselves play? The situation of persecution and martyrdom now universally enforced throughout the Roman Empire of the second to early fourth centuries is, without a doubt, a major contributing factor. The visions of the martyrs provided the suffering Christian communities with the desired encouragement and affirmation of the promised glory awaiting them after death. However, might there be more? Is it possible that the significance and popularity of the visions of the martyrs was due largely to the authority of visions as a God-initiated act over which authorities (church and otherwise) had no control? And, might their popularity also lie in the rich metaphorical and symbolic content of the visions which easily lent themselves to interpretations that may have better reflected emerging theological views of the lay populace? Finally, might the importance and significance of these visions truly lie in their ability, at times, to challenge the prevailing social, ecclesial/religious and sometimes theologically oppressive views?[5] The answers to these questions will prove that the visions of the martyrs did more than just encourage the persecuted church—that they both provided the building blocks for, and inspired, a kind of "popular theology" reflective of its particular historical and theological contexts.

This study will reconstruct from the visions of the martyrs of the second to early fourth centuries what it believes to be a "popular theology" that may not have always conformed to accepted social and theological norms. I refer to the presence of this incongruence with the prevailing Gentile and/or Christian religious and socio-political thought and practice of Graeco-Roman times as "subversive dimensions" of the visions of the martyrs. Also, this study aims at understanding how the situations of persecution and martyrdom and the social, ecclesial, and/or political status of the seer(s)/recorder(s) may have influenced their understanding and interpretation of the visions.

As a means for comparing and identifying any nuances that may arise, the genre of martyrological-hagiography, specifically the literary structure of some visions, will be considered in tandem with the particular visionary texts chosen.

Because of the enormous task of researching and classifying prophetic visions, inside and outside of Christianity, I have limited this survey to those visions within the history of formative Christianity[6] and the emerging catholic Christianity, specifically, to visions of the martyrs of the second to early fourth centuries.

In brief, this study will show that the visions of the martyrs, when interpreted in relation to the visionary/recorder and their socio-cultural political context, reveal a nuanced view of, for example, God, the world, power and powerlessness, death and life that at times subverts what seems to have been construed as normal or dominant by either church or the Graeco-Roman society. Further, this nuanced view reflects what I believe is an underlying grass-roots or popular theology not readily available to the reader through other early church literature.

In support of the aforementioned thesis, I propose the following considerations regarding the significance of visions for the early church. They will be further substantiated (I have alluded to some of them in the body of this essay) as the book develops. They include the following: 1) the authority of prophetic visions as (a) a God-initiated act over which authorities (church and otherwise) had no control, and (b) as divine occurrences receiving multiple attestations throughout the Scriptures and through the people's own freedom and disposition to believe them; 2) the *content* of the visions as affirming or countering dominant beliefs, paradigms, structures; 3) the chosenness or the elective aspect of the *persons* receiving the vision(s) as having nothing to do with social, ecclesiastical status or gender; and 4) the nature of their transcendental truth(s) as transforming power throughout the life of the people of the early church. These presuppositions underlie and will support the development of the argument for the subversive dimension of visions.

# Definitions

## 1) Confessor or Martyr: Defining Who Is a Martyr

To whom do we refer when we speak of "martyr?" What is the difference between confessor and martyr? The word *martyr* comes from the Greek word *mártys* which means witness. Tertullian at an early date applied the term primarily to those Christians who chose to lay down their lives for the faith. According to Edelhard L. Hummel[7] this included those who, after an oral confession of their faith, were soon to suffer death after imprisonment; and/or those who later regained their freedom. In distinguishing between Tertullian's use of *confessor* and *martyr,* Hummel concludes that Tertullian's overall emphasis was to grant the title of martyr only to those Christians who had suffered torture and death for their faith.[8]

Cyprian, an avid reader of the works of Tertullian, further develops and delimits the meaning of the word *martyr* and *confessor.*[9] By the end of the Decian persecution in 251 CE, the word *confessor* is further attenuated. In his book, *The Concept of Martyrdom According to St. Cyprian*, Hummel points to the plethora of primary evidence substantiating Cyprian's development of the meaning of *confessor* and his distinction between *confessor* and *martyr*. According to Hummel, Cyprian distinguished between two types of confessions of faith--a *public* and a *private* confession. The first was made before a pagan official and was usually followed by imprisonment. The other consisted in "taking refuge in prudent flight."[10] More importantly for the purposes of this thesis is his definition of *martyr*, which, given the purpose and consequences of the Decian persecution (249-251), attains a more widened, more comprehensive perspective.

Decius was an old-style Roman who believed that Rome's success and prosperity were integrally connected to the worship of the pagan gods. Early in his reign he initiated a religious campaign to restore Rome to its ancient glory and to consolidate the empire under traditional Roman virtues and beliefs. His goal was not to create martyrs of the Christians but apostates, that is, to acquire from each a formal acknowledgment of the Roman gods. Thus, after the persecution those who had confessed Christ, survived imprisonment and/or torture, returned home. Were these martyrs or confessors?

Given the new circumstances, Cyprian uses the word *martyr* to reflect a more inclusive, perhaps even subversive meaning. Contrary to Decius' desire not to create martyrs, Cyprian uses the term *martyr* to refer to those confessors who, because of their extreme suffering (e.g. relegated to slaving in the mines or mistreatment in prison) were presumed to be proximate to death, as well as to refer to confessors who had undergone suffering *(passio corporis)* and had consummated or 'perfected' their confession through martyrdom (*martyres consummati*). In his letter to his flock at Carthage, for example, Cyprian refers to Aurelius, whom he had raised to the position of lector because of his unrelenting steadfastness under torture, by the term *martyr*:

> Apply yourselves [the church] diligently to prayer, and support our prayers through your own, that in His gracious mercy the Lord may restore to His people unscathed its priest (referring to himself), and with him, the *martyr* and lector.[11]

In another of his letters, Cyprian bids the Carthaginian church to be diligent concerning the bodies of those Christians who had died as a result of their imprisonment.[12] Although they did not suffer torture, their deaths were nevertheless deemed "glorious."[13] Their "courage and honor," Cyprian writes, "is not the less, so as to hinder their being admitted into the company of the blessed martyrs....He who hath offered him[her]self to torture and to death under the Eyes of God, has suffered whatever he was willing to suffer. For he [or she] was not wanting to torture, but the torture to him."[14] For this reason, Cyprian admonished that their departure should also be celebrated among the commemoration of the martyrs.[15]

In the end then, what mattered most was not the "manner" of death, but the believer's "willingness and confession"[16] of faith. Their final "termination by death" was but the last step toward perfecting the glory of martyrdom. Thus, for Cyprian, a martyr was one who, while suffering imprisonment may or may not have incurred death as a result.[17]

Karl Rahner posits three important criteria that prove helpful to the present task of distinguishing the true martyr. According to Rahner, the martyr is one who has suffered a "death which is *violent*, which could have been avoided and which is, nevertheless in freedom...." In his definition, and in opposition to Cyprian, real "death" or a "violent" death (vs. the threat or proximity of death) is the definitive criterion.[18] The title of "martyr" hinges on the realization of the death of the one who chose martyrdom over life. The other key criterion is "freedom," or the ability to *choose* between expressing one's commitment to Christ and apostatizing. The reference to making such a choice (i.e. choosing a death that "could have been avoided") finds ample attestation within the *Acts of the Martyrs*. In his letter to the Romans, for example, Ignatius says that he is "corresponding with all the churches and bidding them all realize that I am *voluntarily* dying for God--if, that is, you do not interfere."[19] Though before our period of study, this letter portrays the importance *choice* played as a defining criterion. Of most consequence, however, is the reference to choice made in connection to Jesus' own death. After being arrested Jesus is brought before Pilate who asks him, "Do you not know that I have the power to release you and the power to crucify you?" Jesus answered: "You would have no power over me whatever unless it were given you from above" (John 19:10-11). According to the Gospel of St. John, Jesus' predicament, including Pilate's "power" to crucify him was pre-ordained by God. "No one," therefore, "takes" Jesus' life from him, "but I lay it down of myself. I have the power to lay it down and the power to take it again" (John 10:17-18). Jesus has *chosen* to suffer martyrdom for the sake of his own (John 10:11, 14).

That the martyr's life is given up freely as a matter of choice (i.e. in persecution) and not "taken" from her/him is made especially clear in the martyrdom of Perpetua. In describing the last events of her martyrdom, the narrator says of Perpetua, "she took the trembling hand of the young gladiator and guided it to her throat. It was as though so great a woman, feared as she was by the unclean spirit, could not be dispatched unless she herself were willing."[20]

This study depends on Cyprian's definition of martyr and Rahner's criteria of freedom. Hence, the term "martyr" will refer to those Christians of the second to fourth centuries who, given the choice between confessing Christ and apostatizing, willingly chose to confess Christ, underwent suffering, and consummated their confession through their death or proximate death.

## 2) Revelation, Vision, Apparition

The definition which follows is purposely broad and simple. David E. Aune's study on visions shows the futility in distinguishing among different types of visions, especially as these "refinements often contribute little to understanding or defining the genre."[21]

In my search, I found that the definition of *revelation* and *vision* overlap. For example, *vision* is defined as "a supernatural appearance that conveys a *revelation.*"[22] *Revelation*, on the other hand, is defined as an "uncovering" or "an act of revealing or communicating divine truth."[23] This definition, however, can easily apply to *visions* also. It seems to me that the difference between *revelation* and *vision* is one of *means*. "Revelation," as defined by Richard P. McBrien, is "the self-communication of God."[24] This self-communication, he adds, is always mediated. "Vision" can thus be defined as a *means* through which this self-communication, or revelation, is mediated. Hence, vision is a *form* of revelation.

In the Christian Scriptures, *revelations* and *visions* are mentioned as separate events. For example, Paul speaks of having "visions and revelations of the Lord" (2 Cor. 12:1). For formative Christianity as well as for the early Christian writers, revelation is "simply the Good News of salvation. Christ is its supreme herald and embodiment, and the prophets, Apostles and Church are its messengers."[25]

The Martyrdoms or *passiones* that concern this study refer only to visions that, at times, also contain *apparitions*. The term *apparitions* is defined as "an unusual or unexpected sight" or "a ghostly figure."[26] An example of an apparition is found in the *Martyrdom of Potamiaena and Basilides* where Potamiaena appears to Basilides after her martyrdom, crowns him and speaks to him. Because of the difficulty in distinguishing between a *vision* and an *apparition*, for the purposes of this study, an apparition will be treated as a vision.

## Martyrdoms within the Scope of this Study

This study relies especially on the *actas* collected and translated by Herbert Anthony Musurillo in *The Acts of the Christian Martyrs*.[27] His book does not include Acts of the Syriac and Persian martyrs which, like this study, fall outside its limits. Since it is the relation of visions to context that is of interest to me, I have simply chosen the martyrdoms with visions that are in this volume.

### 1) The Martyrdom of Perpetua and Felicitas

The *Martyrdom of Perpetua and Felicitas* is among the earliest of the Acts. It is also among the most influential.[28] It has been dated at c. 202/203 during the reign of Septimus Severus. It contains four visions; Perpetua has three and Saturus one. The translation of Musurillo, which is based on the longer Latin text overwhelmingly agreed upon by scholars to be earlier than its Greek counterpart, will be used here. A list of critical editions on the Martyrdom of Perpetua and Felicitas is included in the Appendix.

### 2) The Martyrdom of Potamiaena and Basilides

This story is recorded by Eusebius (*Ecclesiastical History* vi. 5). A slightly different account is preserved also in Palladius' *Lausiac History* but the martyrdom is placed under Maximian (286-305). Eusebius, whom Musurillo considers is correct, places it under Severus c. 205/6-210. Potamiaena is an Alexandrian maiden who, after her martyrdom, appears to Basilides, a converted soldier, and others. Musurillo's text is taken from Eusebius, *EH* vi. 5.

### 3) The Martyrdom of Marian and James

Although some scholars have serious doubts about the authenticity of this *passio*, I include it here because of its popularity (it was known to St. Augustine see *Sermo* 284) and because, according to Musurillo, it reached its final form within the fourth century (c. 300).

James was a deacon and Marian was a lector. Both are martyred in 259 under the second edict of Valerian. During their martyrdom they see a series of prophetic visions reminiscent of the *Martyrdom of Perpetua and Felicitas* (5, 6, 7, 8).[29]

### 4) The Martyrdom of Montanus and Lucius

This martyrdom falls under the second edict of Valerian in the year 259 which was aimed at the clergy. Both are from Carthage. The *passio* is divided in two parts, the first of which recounts the visions they have experienced while in prison. The second part relates the martyrs' deaths and comes from the hand of a disciple of Flavian.[30] According to Musurillo (p. xxxv), the degree of historicity remains a difficult challenge.[31]

This *passio* too is reminiscent of the *Martyrdom of Perpetua and Felicitas*. I will be interested in seeing what visions, symbols/signs, etc. are highlighted and why.[32]

## Procedure

There are many ways to explore visions including, for instance, the disciplines of literature, theology, psychology, history, sociology. This study focuses on visions as a *historical* and *theological* phenomenon. It will not concern itself with the psychological status of visions. Further, we will only consider visions of the martyrs of the Roman empire of the second and early fourth centuries. The definitions of who is a martyr and what is a vision have been delineated above.

We will concentrate on two primary aspects--the *content* of the visions in relation to the visionary/recorder's particular social (e.g. status, gender, age), political, ecclesial (e.g. clergy, layperson, deacon, virgin, celibate, widow) and theological (e.g. Montanism) *contexts*. In other words, we will explore the content of the visions within their own proper historical and theological contexts.

We will also study the texts described below within their own literary context or genre, that is, within the Christian martyrological-hagiography of the times, specifically those containing passion narratives with visions. This study, however, will not isolate nor define the various genres present in the Acts of the Martyrs. As Gary A. Bisbee has already argued, this is an audacious task that would require tracing the origin and development of each genre, including the influence of non-Christian genres.[33] Also, it will not attempt to distinguish between the different types of visions (e.g. apparitions, dreams) as this task has produced little "to the understanding or defining of the genre."[34] Attention to what scholarship says concerning the literary structure of the particular documents in question, however, may provide a point for comparison as well as help assess the significance of common and/or uncommon themes, symbols, and metaphors. This study aims to contribute to that body of knowledge. Finally, studying the production and transmission of the passion narratives with visions will shed light upon the import of these documents upon emerging catholic Christianity.

After a critical analysis of the visions vis-à-vis its contexts--historical, theological and, to some extent, literary--I will be ready to explore and argue for the presence of subversive activity within the visions of the martyrs.[35] Subversive activity will be defined as that (within the visions) which challenges, contradicts or is incongruent with what the study of the theological and historical contexts showed to be dominant, or normal. Careful attention will be given to the *symbols*, *images*, *metaphors*, the *signs*[36] inherent in the visions. When studied against their contexts, how might these have been subversive? And of whom? or what? Was there, for example, a double-meaning intended--a type of encoding meant for a select group? Who would have understood these signs? What are the religious and or cultural codes that would help the reader unlock the meaning(s) referenced by these signs and thus arrive at their subversive nature? This analysis, in conjunction with the results of the survey of the social, political, ecclesial, and theological categories, should provide: 1) new and interesting information regarding the subversive role of the visions of martyrs in relation to the social political, ecclesial order of the times and, 2) the historical and theological basis for arguing on behalf of an underlying grass-roots or popular theology as reflected in the visions of the martyrs of the Roman empire of the second to early fourth centuries.

In *St. Martin de Porres: The "Little Stories" and the Semiotics of Culture*,[37] Alex García-Rivera provides a method which will aid the development of this thesis. This three-part method (perspective, structure, and dynamics) provides many of the clues toward assessing the nature and degree (if any) of subversion in the visions of the martyrs. In part A of this section, I present his method in the form of questions that will guide my research. Part B includes other equally important questions, not directly stemming from his method, that relate to the social situation and agenda in the production and transmission of the documents. These questions will help to locate issues of status, class, race and entitlement.

# Questions That Will Serve as Clues

(I use the *Martyrdom of Perpetua and Felicitas* below for the purpose of illustration.)

### What Are the Obvious and Not-So Obvious Signs?

How common were these signs? Who would/not have understood them? 2) What are the recurrent metaphors? 3) Are there any kinds of binary oppositions? And, are they recurrent? Are binary oppositions reversed? How are they illustrated? Binary oppositions, (e.g. cold versus hot, in versus out, death versus life,) point to semiotic boundaries that, should they be crossed or united, will aid in determining the role and nature of subversive activity/interpretation.[38]

For example, an interesting binary opposition occurs in the visions of Perpetua, between "milk" and "cheese," between liquid and solid. (We know that a child must drink milk but an adult can take the milk in solid form as cheese. What is this telling us and how might it be related to Perpetua?) 4) What are the codes at work? "How were things done?"[39] Or, What is the "norm?" (For instance, how were women viewed in the third and fourth centuries?) This includes the presence of code reversals in which, for example, women fight gladiators and win.[40] 5) "Are binary oppositions being compared? Are certain binary oppositions being reversed? Do the mighty now bow down and are the lowly raised high?"[41]

### Other Important Questions

The following questions (not included in García-Rivera's method) relate to social situation and agenda in the production and transmission of the documents. They also help to locate issues of status, class, race and entitlement. 1) How does the life-situation (e.g. status, gender) of the martyr influence the subversiveness of the vision? 2) How did the martyr's prophetic vision(s) inform, subvert, alter prevailing ideas on subjectivity--how did they challenge (a) society's concept of social arrangements? (e.g. who is capable of being a subject?), b) ecclesiastical concept(s) of, for example, gender, equality, holiness? 3) Who wrote the *passio*? 4) Were they popular literature or theological literature? Were they inside ("orthodox") or outside (heterodox) the Church? 5) Who transcribed the visions and why?

## Description of Contents

Chapter Two provides a historical and theological introduction to the argument and discussion around the subversive dimensions of the visions of the martyrs in the rest of the chapters. Its purpose is to ground the theme within its historical and theological traditions—Hebrew and formative Christianity. It begins with a brief discussion of the importance of the early church understanding of the martyrs' visions as prophetic and, as communal property. The *prophetic* theme leads into the next section--an overview of the role of subversion within the visions of the Hebrew and Christian scriptures. In addition, the definition of subversion, and how it will be used in the rest of the chapters, is further discussed and delimited.

Chapter Three explores the early church's understanding of the role and function of the Acts of the Martyrs. In particular it will show how the visions contained therein not only helped to define how the Acts were used, they also worked together as a subversive force against the church's oppressors (i.e. the Roman state).

Chapter Four locates and defines subversive elements within two visions: the vision of the bishop Polycarp and the vision of Saturus in the Martyrdom of Perpetua and Felicitas. For the purposes of this chapter, I have isolated a portion of Saturus' vision for analysis (Musurillo 121, ch. 13.1-8). The following reasons justify this step: 1) the section in question seems to deviate from whole of the vision, 2) its parenthetical nature has also been noted by other scholars,[42] and 3) the brevity of the events allows for a quick yet powerful example of the presence of subversive elements. I deal with the rest of Saturus' vision in the following chapter.

Chapter Five concentrates on the vision of Saturus. It argues that what is being described in the second or symbolic layer of his vision is a drama of initiation that begins in the arena and ends in the heavenly temple, in the Holy of Holies at the throne of the God-Christ. Further, it argues that this imagery of blood, temple, throne and Christ, defied Jewish atonement theology and reflected ongoing antagonisms between Jews and Christians in Carthage. Finally, it also argues for subversion against the Roman state through the visions' image of Saturus and Perpetua's journey from the arena to the throne; from the margins to the center.

Chapter Six focuses on Perpetua's visions of her deceased brother Dinocrates. Her function as intercessor on behalf of his suffering soul, and her subsequent leadership and ministerial roles are explored and discussed in light of the context of martyrdom. The subversive implications of Perpetua's leadership and ministerial functions end this chapter.

The book ends with a concluding essay summarizing the arguments.

## Notes

1. Herbert Anthony Musurillo, "The Martyrdom of Marian and James," in *The Acts of The Christian Martyrs*, trans. Herbert Anthony Musurillo (Oxford: Clarendon, 1972) 205, ch. 7.5-7.
2. Robert W. Frank, "Visions," *An Encyclopedia of Religion*, 1945 ed.
3. Frank 815.
4. The popularity of this literature is discussed below and will be treated further within the body of this book.
5. I cannot overemphasize that any conclusion on subversive activity within the visions must and will be made in relation to its particular historical and theological contexts. This criterion is imperative to remaining true to the context and to what, at least in theory, was going forward.
6. At the suggestion of Richard Valantasis, with whom I agree, I am using "formative Christianity" to refer to (and describe) the church (including its thoughts, deeds, events, etc.) of the New Testament or first century and, "emerging catholic Christianity" will refer to the church of the 2nd to 4th centuries.
7. In *The Concept of Martyrdom According to St. Cyprian of Carthage*, Hummel surveys various important works on Tertullian's definition of *martyr* and *confessor*. He also points to the later development of the title of "martyr," as delimited by the Montanist Tertullian, to refer to those who had undergone death for Christ. In distinguishing between Tertullian's use of *confessor* and *martyr*, Hummel concludes that Tertullian's overall emphasis was to grant the title of "martyr" to those Christians who had suffered torture and death for their faith (see especially Tertullian's last work, *De Pudicitia* [22]). (Washington: Catholic University of America Press, 1946) 1-5.
8. Hummel 1-5.
9. In support, Hummel cites St. Jerome's *De Viris Inlustribus* 53 and other works. See also p. 3, n. 11.
10. *secundus ad gloriam gradus est caute secessione subtractum iam Deo reservari.* In Hummel 11. He cites Cyprian's *De Lapsis*, ch. 3.
11. Italics mine. *Vos orationibus frequenter insistite et preces nostras vestris precibus adiuvate, ut Domini misericordia favens nobis cito plebi suae et sacerdotem reddat incolumem et martyrem cum sacerdote lectorem.Epistle* 38. See also *Epistle* 66, 4 (*Corpus Scriptorum Ecclesiasticorum Latinorum* 3.2.729, 13 Hartel) and Epistle 76 (CSEL 3.2.827, 15-17 Hartel) both also cited in Hummel 8,9. English translation by Hummel.
12. *The Epistles of S. Cyprian, Bishop of Carthage and Martyr, with The Council of Carthage on Baptism of Heretics, To Which are Added, The Extant Works of S. Pacian, Bishop of Barcelona*, ed. E. B. Pusey, John Keble, J. H. Newman, C. Marriott (Oxford: Parker, 1844), 30.
13. *The Epistles* 30.
14. *The Epistles* 30.
15. *The Epistles* 30.
16. *The Epistles* 30. See also Hummel 14-27.

17. Christians who were imprisoned (or exiled) but did not suffer torture or mistreatment were called "confessors." See Hummel 14-20. Cyprian also speaks of a kind of 'spiritual martyrdom.' See Hummel 9 and 20-27. This study will not endeavor into these distinctions.

18. This criterion is also explicit in Origen's "Exhortation to Martyrdom." See *The Classics of Western Spirituality*, trans. Rowan A. Greer (New York: Paulist, 1979) 41-79.

19. *Early Christian Fathers*, ed. and trans. Cyril C. Richardson (New York: Collier, 1970) 105.

20. "The Martyrdom of Perpetua and Felicitas," in Musurillo 127.

21. David E. Aune, *Prophecy in Early Christianity and the Ancient Mediterranean World* (Grand Rapids: Eerdmans, 1983) 99. See also note 147 on p. 373 of his book.

22. *Webster's Seventh New Collegiate Dictionary*, (Springfield: Merriam, 1969) 994. (Italics mine).

23. *Webster's* 735.

24. Richard P. McBrien, *Catholicism* (San Francisco: Harper, 1994) 264.

25. *Catholicism* 270.

26. *Webster's* 42.

27. (Oxford: Clarendon, 1972). Musurillo's book is a collection of twenty-eight of the *actas*. It also contains a useful introduction regarding the state of scholarship regarding the historical/literary nature of the *actas* and provides an introduction to each of the narratives. His method of selection includes reliability and/or the importance and instructiveness of the document(s). To decide the importance and instructiveness of a text Musurillo depends on the amount of information the document reveals about the nature of the early church and its times. His book does not include Acts of the Syriac and Persian martyrs which, like this study, falls outside its limits. Other critical editions include: E. C. E. Owen, *Some Authentic Acts of the Early Martyrs* (Oxford, 1927). Musurillo, who cites Owen, considers his translation of thirteen of the *Acts* and his notes very useful; Hugo Rahner, *Die Märtyrerakten des zweiten Fahrhunderts* (Freiburg i.B., 1954). Rahner translates seven of the earliest *actas* and provides an extensive and useful introduction (pp. 1-22); Daniel Ruíz Bueno, intro. annotations and trans. *Actas de los Mártires* (Madrid: Editorial Católica, 1968) which contains both the Latin or Greek and the Spanish translation; and K. Lake and J. E. L. Oulton (Eng. trans.,intro. and notes), *Eusebius, Bishop of Caesarea, The Ecclesiastical History and Martyrs of Palestine*, 2 vols. (London, 1928, reprinted 1954). I will be using Musurillo's collection as a representative sample.

28. On Augustine's use of the *Acta* in his sermon see W. H. Shewring, *The Passion of S. S. Perpetua and Felicity MM. together with the Sermons of S. Augustine upon these Saints* (London: Sheed, 1931) 45-59.

29. The text used by Musurillo, upon which I will rely, is taken from P. Franchi de' Cavalieri, 'Passio SS. Mariani et Iacobi,' *Studi e Testi* 3 (Rome, 1900)47-61. Cavalieri uses ten manuscripts but relies chiefly on A, codex Augustodunensis 34, from the Seminary Library at Autun, France (s. ix). See also Thierry Ruinart, *Acta martyrum*, 268-74; Lazzati, *Gli suiluppi*, 190-200.

30. For more information on Flavian see Musurillo xxxv.

31. For a short argument see Musurillo xxxv.

32. The text used by Musurillo is adapted from P. Franchi de' Cavalieri, 'Gli Attti dei SS. Montano, Lucio e compagni,' *Römische Quartalschrift* 8, Supplementheft (1898)71-86, and 'Nuove osservazione critiche ed esegetiche sul testo della Passio Sanctorum Montani et Lucii' in *Note agiografiche, fas. 3,' Studi e Testi* 22 (1909) 3-31. For the manuscripts cited by Cavalieri see Musurillo, xxxvi. See also Ruinart, *Acta martyrum*, 275-82 and Lazzati, *Gli suiluppi*, 201-13.

33. Bisbee 5.
34. Aune 99 and note 147.
35. I understand that I may find that some visions or parts thereof, may in fact support prevailing views on, for instance, the meaning of martyrdom, life and death. This will also constitute part of my findings.
36. Augustine, considered by many to be "the greatest semiotician of antiquity and the real founder of semiotics," defined *sign* as "a thing which, over and above the impression it makes on the senses, causes something else to come into the mind as a consequence of itself." Simply stated, a sign is "*everything* that can be taken as *something serving for something else.*" Or "*everything* that, on the grounds of a previously established social [and ecclesial] convention can be taken as *something standing for something else.*" Umberto Eco, *A Theory of Semiotics* (Bloomington: Indiana UP, 1979) 16. See Augustine's *De doctrina christiana* 2.1.1 (written in 397 CE). Augustine's theory of signs is also developed in his *De magistro* (389) and *Principia dialectical* (c. 384). For more information on Augustine's semiotic theory see Winfied Noth, *Handbook of Semiotics* (Indianapolis: Indiana UP, 1990) 15.
37. I have found his book extremely helpful in elucidating the role and use of semiotics, specifically in terms of culture. See pp. 36-39 (Maryknoll, New York: Orbis Books, 1995). Semiotics is "a science that studies the life of signs within society." Saussure de Ferdinand as quoted in Noth 3.
38. For more on the nature and role of binary oppositions to semiotic boundaries see García-Rivera 36-37.
39. Garcia-Rivera 38.
40. See the *Martyrdom of Perpetua and Felicitas*.
41. García-Rivera 38.
42. Robeck 83 and Petraglio 28-9.

# Chapter 2

# The Visions of the Martyrs and the Role of Subversion

Visions, though directly related to the visionary's questions and situation, were nevertheless believed by the martyr and the church to address not just the martyr, but the church community as a whole.[1] Two major events in the life of the church help explain this phenomenon. One pertains to their *historical* context and the other to a *theological* development. This chapter looks briefly at how these contexts influenced the emerging church's understanding of the martyrs' visions as prophetic. Also, how this view reinforced the authority and influence of their visions.

## The Visions of the Martyrs as Communal Property

The situation of persecution and martyrdom and the subsequent need for the church to look to the witness of their martyrs for strength and encouragement, provides the critical historical dimension to understanding the early church's view of the martyrs' visions as communal property. The witness of the martyrs and their visions were needed to strengthen the Christian's decision to seek to remain firm within a religion that by outside standards (e.g. Hebrew religion, Graeco-Roman state and pagan religions) was, more often than not, viewed as a superstitious and subversive anomaly.[2] (More will be said regarding the function of visions amidst persecution in Chapter Three.) The second, is the identification of the martyr as prophet.[3] The Hebrew idea that "every prophet was believed to be a martyr...every martyr a prophet"[4] gained particular expression within Christianity in times of persecution. This analogy between the martyr-prophet is ingrained in the martyrological-hagiographical accounts of the martyrs' death.[5] Among the evidence used in these accounts to support this analogy, is the martyr's experience of visions. In his book, *The Martyrs: A Study in Social Control*, Donald W. Riddle correctly argues that martyrs were not only venerated, but that "the abilities of the apostles were ascribed to them," the charism of prophecy, especially through visions, "being the most valued of these."[6] According to Violet MacDermot, the essential characteristic of the saints was not their power to effect miracles but their ability to see visions and communicate with the divine world.[7] The experience of visions testified to the martyrs' "prophetic faculties."[8] Because visions were considered prophetic, they were deemed communal property--the common heritage of the church.

The third, and probably the most important aspect influencing the early church belief in the communal ownership of the martyrs' visions, is their theological understanding of the "church" as "one body" with "one faith" and "one baptism" (Eph. 4:4,5). This view, found early on in Paul's analogy of the church as the "body of Christ,"[9] is by the third and fourth century church metamorphosed into an understanding of the martyr as a faithful representative of that body whose visions were thus intended for the whole community.

In conclusion, the for early Christian, there was no sense of a merely private vision, no conception of private encouragement not also intended to stimulate and strengthen the whole. As a result, visions were shared with fellow Christians on their way to martyrdom and most were recorded and passed on from church community to church community, and interpreted and reinterpreted throughout Christendom.

In the Hebrew Scriptures, the identification of the martyr with the prophet carried subversive implications. Is this also true for the visions of the Christian martyrs? A historical and theological overview of the Hebrew and Christian subversive tradition follows.

# A Historical Overview of the Subversive Dimensions of Visions from the Hebrew Scriptures to Formative Christianity

Despite the exalted nature of their calling, prophets were not always esteemed; nor were their prophetic messages welcome. King Ahab, for example, called the prophet Elijah a "disturber of Israel" (I Kings 18:17) and sought to kill him. Disturbing Israel seemed to be a common trend among prophets whose messages almost always challenged the political and religious powers of the times (e.g. Amos 5:9-15 speaks against social injustices and religious practices; Jeremiah protests against a false sense of security that shows itself in the blatant neglect of the needy, injustices and pagan worship 7:1-7; Isaiah protests against Israel's "adulteress" behavior and prophesied concerning God's judgment against Zion 1:21-31; 3:1-4:1). This challenge took the form of "dissent" and subversion.[10] That is, their message not only went against the current patterns of behavior and/or thought but actually upset or overturned them.

By the mid-second century, early Christianity's view of the prophet had undergone some change. Not only is the martyr considered a prophet (see above), s/he is also highly esteemed and revered for her/his participation in the suffering and death of Christ through martyrdom.[11] This *imitatio Christi*, however, is not without its own subversive dimensions, as we shall see below. And, as with the Hebrew prophets, subversion becomes especially explicit through their prophetic message(s) vis-à-vis their life/death.

The visions of the martyrs, when studied in relation to their context, reveal the continuation of the prophetic tradition of dissent and subversion, that is, of upsetting, undercutting or reversing things as they are for things as they should be.

One might rightly argue that visions, because of their presumed divine origin, and because neither the state nor the Christian church could preclude the experience, rule the content, nor delimit the choice of its recipients, were of themselves subversive. This can be seen, for instance, in the account of Stephen's martyrdom (Acts 7:54-60). Through his death, the Pharisees could prevent him from ever preaching about Christ. However, they could not stop divine prerogative from choosing Stephen over the Pharisees to reveal divine glory (Acts 7:55).[12] Further, the nature of martyrdom itself as a subversive act against the state and the dominant pagan culture is acknowledged. For instance, Eusebius (c. 260-c. 340) reflects this view in his account of four women who, despite being severely tortured, would not give in to the governors demand to deny Christ and offer sacrifice. Of the governor, Eusebius says, "[he] was ashamed to ply continued tortures all to no end, and to be worsted [i.e. defeated] by women...."[13] Origen's *Exhortation to Martyrdom* perhaps best captures the subversive role of martyrdom or *imitatio Christi*:

> God, moreover, says by the Prophet: *In an acceptable time I have heard thee, and in the day of salvation I have helped thee.* What time could be more acceptable than when, because of our piety towards God in Christ, we make our solemn entry in this world surrounded by a guard and when we are led out, more like triumphant conquerors than conquered? For martyrs in Christ *despoil* with Him *the principalities and powers* and triumph with Him, by partaking in His sufferings and the great deeds accomplished in His sufferings--among which is His triumphing over principalities and powers, which you will soon see conquered and overcome with shame. What other day could be for us such a day of salvation as the day of so glorious a departure from here below?[14]

Origen's inversion of "conqueror" and "conquered" and his reference to despoiling "the principalities and powers" is indicative of the nature and degree of subversion inherent in the actions of the martyr-prophet. Martyrdom is, for the believer, "the day of salvation"; death is subverted by new life, power by powerlessness and the world (or below) by the triumph of Christ's death and resurrection in which the martyr participates.

On occasion (as they did with Israel), the messages and actions of the martyr-prophets also upset the church's teachings. One such occasion is related to the church's espousal and promotion of the dominant patriarchal values shared by Jews and Gentiles toward the beginning of the second century.[15] By this time, women's social and religious roles were relegated and intricately tied to procreation and motherhood.[16] Addressing the extent of acculturation to the dominant culture, Clarissa W. Atkinson points out that writings, for example, that contained and exalted egalitarianism in gender relations (as characterized by the Jesus movement of the first century) were slowly excluded from the scriptural canon. However, she clarifies that the egalitarian view was not totally eradicated since glimpses of this eschatological vision of equality were preserved in certain Pauline passages and other writings such as, the Apocryphal Acts and the Acts of the Martyrs.[17] While the Apocryphal Acts became marginalized along with other "heterodox" texts, the Acts of the Martyrs "held a central place in doctrine and devotion."[18] Most importantly, Atkinson points out that:

> during the long period of persecution preceding the establishment of Christianity in the fourth century, *martyrdom* and persecution undercut the values of the dominant culture, breaking traditional [patriarchal] bonds and forging new ones. Faced with violent, immediate death, the martyrs recreated the family of discipleship modeled by the men and women who followed Jesus to his crucifixion. In many respects they shared the voice and vision of the disciples as well as their experience of *communitas*.[19]

She further argues that "these Acts present very different models of family and of gender relations; they demonstrate the martyr's renunciation of traditional concerns and reversal of ordinary priorities."[20]

As shown above, the argument for the subversive role of martyrdom itself is firmly attested. However, there is much more to be said about the nature and degree of subversion that can be discovered only through the careful analysis of the *content* of the visions of the martyrs in comparison with the prevailing religious and socio-political *contexts* of the times.[21] How are these visions subversive, that is, upsetting, undercutting or reversing things as they are for things as they should be? And who or what is being subverted? How does the content and context aid our understanding of the nature and degree of subversion? The Christian scriptures provide us with various examples and answers to these questions.

Just before his death, the deacon Stephen, experiences a vision that subverts the prevailing socio-religious notions of life and death, of power and powerlessness. His vision of Jesus' (the "Son of Man") exalted position at the right hand of God (Acts 7:56) challenged Hebrew understandings of Jesus as a false prophet whose existence was terminated at the criminal's cross. This intimate revelation of the glory awaiting him at his departure from this life--his place of destination, also challenged dominant notions of power.[22] The accuser's power to take life is surpassed by God's power not only to give life but, *eternal* life, with Him. Most important for the developing church of the first four centuries, Stephen's experience provided a *visual* affirmation[23] to the counter cultural view first articulated and modeled by Jesus that "Whoever would preserve his life will lose it, but whoever loses his life for my sake and the gospel's will preserve it" (Mk 8:35).

This subversive view of life and death would find expression in the fertile ground of the persecution and martyrdom of early Christians. And, the martyrs' visions offer a compelling window into the nature and extent of this and other subversive dimensions.

In one of his visions, Paul says that he was "snatched up to Paradise to hear words which cannot be uttered, words which no person may speak" (2 Cor. 12: 1-4). Though very little information is given, the choice of words used to describe his experience is telling. From this description the reader is able to make at least two important observations. First, Paul's use of the word "Paradise" to describe what he saw sets up binary opposition between it and the "world," that is, between "paradise" and earthly existence. The state's use of suffering and the threat of death to create apostates assume the primacy of earthly existence. The opposition between "paradise" and his earthly existence implies the contrary (the primacy of eternal life with God in paradise) and, the stress on the unutterability of the words he heard strengthens the depth of this opposition (e.g. the words are inexpressible because they refer to things unlike anything he has experienced in this world.) The significance and import of this vision and the opposition it sets up are further solidified through Paul's later statement, "For, to me, 'life' means Christ; hence dying is so much gain" (Phil. 1:21). Once again, and within the context of martyrdom, visions function to subvert any action aimed at undermining Christian views of life and death, power and powerlessness.

Another example of the subversive dimension in the visions of the martyrs is found in the book of Revelation where the author, who had been exiled to the island of Patmos because he "proclaimed God's word and bore witness to Jesus," experiences an array of visions (Rev. 1:9). His visions not only served to strengthen him during his own persecution, they were also aimed at encouraging the faithful through visions revealing the imminent end of their suffering and the proximity of a new reign of peace and justice. The powerful effect of these visions against impending death is heard in John of Patmos' subversive statement, "happy is the person who reads this prophetic message, and happy are those who hear and heed what is written in it, for the appointed time is near!" (Rev 1:3).[24]

As shown above, sufficient evidence exists on behalf of the role of subversion in the visions of the martyrs of formative Christianity and, as will be explored, in the visions of the martyrs of the church of the second to early fourth centuries. The term *subversion* has been defined in light of the relation between the *content* of the vision and the *context* and refers to that which upsets, undercuts or reverses "things as they are" for things "as they should be." "Things as they are" will sometimes be referred to as the dominant paradigm, the norm or prevailing context (e.g. behavior, thought, attitude). Things "as they should be" will refer to that new way of being, thinking or seeing that is portrayed through the visions and which goes against the prevailing norm.

It is important to remember that the visions were had within the context of martyrdom. Stories about this context became engraved in the early church literature called the Acts of the Martyrs. These stories not only framed the visions, they also provided the reader with clues that helped unlock the meaning(s) of the visions. Together, the Acts of the Martyrs and the visions they framed, powerfully undermined their oppressors. The next chapter explores this relationship and its subversive implications.

# Notes

1. Evidence that their function as communal property aimed, for example, at "the consolation of the church" is affirmed through Augustine's use and mention of them in his sermon on Perpetua and her companions, on Crispina of Thagora, and the Forty Martyrs. See Augustine, Sermo 280 in *Patrologia Latina*, ed. J. P. Migne (Paris, 1844-64) 38:1281; Tertullian, De anima 55.4 in *Corpus Christianorum*, ed. J. H. Waszink (1954) 861. 32.

2. This is not to say that many Christians did not 'apostatize' during persecution.

3. The tradition likening the martyr to a prophet has precedence in Jewish and Christian scriptures and literature. For a discussion on Hebrew and Christian (and some Hellenistic) sources referring to the role of the prophet as martyr and the prophetic role of martyrs see H. A. Fischel, "Martyr and Prophet: A Study in Jewish Literature," Jewish Quarterly Review 37 (1946/47): 364-370. In the early second-century document, the Didache (or the Teaching of the Twelve Apostles), the author(s)'s exhortation regarding the "true" and "false" prophet provides several important guidelines which the martyr-prophet embodied to the fullest extent. First, the writer sets parameters by which the true "prophet" is distinguished from the false prophet. The most important of these is their "conduct," that is, a prophet practices what s/he preaches (ch. 11.8). This qualification would be directly related to and fulfilled by the martyr-prophet who gave (or was about to give) her/his life as witness to their faith. The document also exhorts its readers against prophets who would ask or accept "anything save sufficient food to carry him till the next lodging (ch. 11.6)." In accordance with this rule, the martyr-prophet did not demand anything but the privilege of self-sacrifice. In *Early Christian Fathers*, ed. Cyril C. Richardson (New York: Macmillan, 1970) 161-179. Although the document was addressed to rural Christian communities in Syria-Palestine, its popularity and authority were such that it was regarded by many as pertaining to canonical literature prior to the end of the fourth century.

The issue of credulity as dependent on the prophet's life is also taken up by Roland E. Murphy's essay, "Prophets and Wise Men as Provokers of Dissent," in *The Right to Dissent*, eds. Hans Küng and Jürgan Moltmann (New York: Seabury, 1982) 61-66.

4. Fischel 1.

5. Fischel includes a list of 24 traits that were used to emphasize the identification of the prophet with the martyr (383-384).

6. Riddle (Chicago: U of Chicago P, 1931) 73. Arguing for his thesis that the deeds of the martyrs were the result of socio-religious control, he adds that "the thought that the martyr obtained this special power had great effect, it would appear, in inducing candidates to undertake the experience....It was of value in inducing the attitude of willingness to undertake martyrdom to assure a potential martyrs that he would, through his experience, achieve the role of prophet." Riddle comes at the study of martyrdom from a sociological perspective which minimizes, to the detriment of the full implication(s) of the study of martyrdom, the role and function of theology in informing and shaping the religious experience. While his study throws important and necessary light on the role of religion in shaping attitudes and controlling behavior, it would be simplistic to assume that this was all that was being signified by the martyr's willingness to die.

In his study regarding the work of the Holy Spirit in contexts of persecution and martyrdom in the New Testament and early church, Weinrich presents and affirms this position. In agreement with and support of Karl Holl and Marc Lod, Weinrich declares that a martyr was "an ecstatic to whom revelations were given. The martyr became a prophet by virtue of a special gift of the Spirit which enabled the martyr to view into the invisible world. In this manner the confessor and martyr became a 'witness' to the resurrected Christ." See p. xii.

7. MacDermot further argues that the visions of the martyrs 'reassured' those who, "unable to create such a world for themselves, might doubt its existence." See *The Cult of the Seer in the Ancient Middle East: A Contribution to Current Research on Hallucinations Drawn form Coptic and Other Texts* (Berkley: U of California P, 1971) 94.

8. Fischel 368.

9. See 1 Cor. 10:17, 12:12-13 and 12:20.

10. On the subject of dissent and the prophetic message see Murphy's essay cited above.

11. This reverence will later lead to their veneration through relics. See Lawrence S. Cunningham, *The Meaning of Saints* (San Francisco: Harper, 1980).

12. The content and significance of Stephen's vision is dealt with further in the pages that follow.

13. This subversive attitude is further reflected in his comment regarding the death of Nemesion. Eusebius states that the governor had ordered Nemesion to be burned between two bandits. The governor's probable intentions of mocking the Christians with a reenactment of Christ's death is subverted by Eusebius' comment that the governor had instead "honor[ed] him--blest indeed!--with a resemblance to Christ." *Eusebius: The Ecclesiastical History and the Martyrs of Palestine*, trans. and notes Hugh Jackson Lawlor and John E. L. Oulton (New York: Macmillan, 1927) 1: VI.41.18.

14. In *Ancient Christian Writers*, trans. John J. O'Meara (New York: Newman P, 1954) 186.

15. See Clarissa Atkinson, *The Oldest Vocation: Christian Motherhood in the Middle Ages* (London: Cornell UP, 1991) 18-19.

16. Atkinson makes an interesting and, I think correct, interpretation of the meaning between, for example, Ignatius' work and instruction regarding the (male) leaders of the church and the further development and institution of patriarchy. She states, "at the beginning of the second century, Ignatius of Antioch instructed Christians to 'regard the bishop as the Lord himself.' Bishops soon became teachers, rulers, and 'fathers'; Ignatius told the Magnesians, whose bishop was a young man, 'to render him all respect according to the power of God the Father.' The patriarchal authority of men was easily conflated with the authority of God and restored to the 'households' of the new churches" (17-18 and notes 26 and 27).

17. Atkinson 19.

18. Atkinson 19.

19. Atkinson 19.

20. Atkinson 18-19. For example, in regards to the Martyrdom of Perpetua and Felicitas, she states, "God facilitated the martyrdom of Perpetua and Felicitas despite their physiological condition. The biological demands of motherhood, accepted in the ancient world as marks and determinants of female incapacity, were not allowed to stand in the way of the martyrs' witness. Motherhood was not in itself redemptive, but neither did it preclude participation in the most sacred vocation" (21-22).

21. I am aware that visions and their interpretations, when given, may be literary creations rather than actual transcriptions or summaries of the visions of the martyrs. This, however, in no way hinders the possibility of studying the visions for their subversive elements vis-à-vis their religious and/or socio-political contexts.

22. In his desire to distance Stephen's vision from the view that it was merely a "typical feature of stories of martyrdom," Weinrich maintains that the vision held no benefit for Stephen and was instead intended for the benefit of the Jewish leaders. His first argument, that the vision held no benefit for Stephen is simply a judgment which is

insubstantiable. That it did not "reveal the future fate of the martyr" is a narrow explanation of the vision and overlooks the theological connection of "the heavens" where God (and Jesus) is with the believer's ultimate 'place' of destination. As Christ died and rose to be with the "Father," so it was taught that the Christian would also die and rise to be with the "Father." It is only in this sense that the vision's prophetic thrust is fully appreciated. Hence, the man that they are about to stone not only has a vision of the glory of God, but, despite their efforts at finishing with his life, their evil actions only serve to precipitate his participation in the glory just revealed to him. (It also serves, as Weinrich points out, to spread the gospel). One cannot but ascertain that the vision does then, reveal something about the martyr's fate!

In his argument for the distinction between early Christian martyr-texts and the vision of Stephen, he uses 'consciousness,' vs. ecstasy or trance, as the line of demarcation. He states "there is no indication that Stephen was in a trance or ecstasy. He was conscious enough to relate on the spot his vision to his hearers" (42). First, one might ask what does "conscious enough" mean? Secondly, while one might agree with him that Stephen's vision was not just another "typical" occurrence related to martyrdom (but then we can also say the same for any other vision), his argument actually serves to place undue emphasis on "mode" rather than on content, the main focus. Furthermore, and in agreement with Violet MacDermot, "distinction between seeing the visions in a state of dream, ecstasy, or trance, and the exercise of the conscious imagination, was not clear to the writers of the Hellenistic or early Christian period" (54). Thus, whether a "vision," or not a vision--in Weinrich's view, we must acknowledge that the recorder understood and recorded it as such. See Weinrich 38-43.

23. The author's proof that Stephen's vision can be trusted as true or real for all believers is based on his reference to the Holy Spirit in him. Thus it states that Stephen was "a man filled with faith and the Holy Spirit....A man filled with grace and power, who worked great wonders and signs among the people." And again before his stoning, it states that Stephen was "filled with the Holy Spirit." See Acts 6:5,8; 7:51.

24. Reference to the "appointed time" meant not only their redemption from oppression, but the avenging of their suffering "when Jesus will return in glory" (note 1:3 in *The New American Bible*, 1970). See also Rev. 12.

# Chapter 3

# Visions and the Acts of the Martyrs

In this chapter I will show how the early church's understanding of the function of the Acts of the Martyrs contributed to their understanding of the function of the visions of the martyrs. I argue that the Acts, and the visions they contained, formed a symbiotic relationship that greatly enhanced the church's ability to cope with the situation of persecution in many ways. Further, that together, the *Acts* and the visions became a dangerous tool, powerfully undermining the persecuting forces.

I begin with a brief overview of the development and transmission of the *Acts*.

## A Subversive Cooperation

The *Acts of the Martyrs* (*acta* or *gesta*, also known as *acta Christianorum*[1]) is a genre of literature that is thought to have begun circulating among the Christian communities in the mid-second century with the *Martyrdom of Polycarp*, if not earlier.[2] According to Gary A. Bisbee, most scholars tend to agree that many of the earliest *acta martyrum* were actually copies of *hypomnematismoi* (*commentarius -i* in Latin*)*, or official court discourses between magistrates and martyrs (e.g. the *Acts of the Scillitan Martyrs,* the *Acts of Justin Martyr*).[3] Many *Acts*, however, also contain *Passiones* (or *martyria*)--stories about the arrest, imprisonment and execution of the martyr that claim to have been written by Christian eyewitnesses, contemporaries, or by the martyr her/himself. For instance, the Martyrdom of Perpetua and Felicitas and also the Martyrdom of Montanus and Lucius purportedly contain autobiographical information together with accounts of their execution written by an eyewitness. In the Martyrdom of Perpetua and Felicitas we have an example of a work that incorporates the three popular hagiographical genres; an eyewitness redaction and narrative (in the form of prologue and epilogue, chs. 1-2 and 14-21), an excerpt from the court hearing (6), and an autobiographical account (11-13). The visions of the martyrs are found in the accounts of their *passiones*.

The *passiones (*as well as many of the *Acts*) was a literature especially written for the church by church people. Lay, as well as clergy, compiled and redacted the stories that would powerfully influence the life and thought of the third and fourth century church, (and beyond). The urgency of the times as well as its story-type narrative contributed to the *passiones'* simple style. However, one scholar notes that "the simplicity of their redaction (i.e. the *Acts* and the *passiones*) had, without a doubt, as much persuasive force as an eloquent panegyric."[4] This simplicity, at times clumsy but sometimes vibrant with colorful and passionate eloquence, contributed to their popularity. Written in the language of the people, about persons they loved and admired for their steadfastness, the *passiones* were dear to their hearts and minds.[5]

According to W. H. C. Frend, the number of *Acts* written, especially during the fourth and fifth centuries reach into the hundreds.[6] In the Martyrology[7] of Carthage alone (each great provincial see had a list of martyrs) Frend records no less than eighty-six entries, each of which contained some information on the arrest, trial and execution of the martyr.[8] The church obtained the *Acts* by various means, including bribing the tribunal agents.[9] Daniel Ruíz Bueno, for example, points out that after the last persecution, the Council of Arles (314) used the public Acts it had acquired to establish who among them were *traditores,* that is, who had turned over the sacred books to Diocletian's soldiers.[10]

The question of the legal basis that led to Christians being arraigned and prosecuted before the reign of Decius and Valerian remains unanswered.[11] "In the provinces, local magistrates, and in Rome the *perfectus urbi*, could, under a variety of charges, prosecute any person who threatened the *pax romanum*."[12] By Diocletian's reign, however, the chief reasons for the aggression felt toward Christians are established. These can be seen in the words attributed to governor Calvisianus in the Martyrdom of Euplus:

> Calvisianus in giving sentence said: The adversaries and enemies of our most mighty gods, men who are not submissive or obedient to our lords the emperors who are for ever to be revered, these deliberately sin against themselves and should be destroyed with dispatch.[13]

This statement intensely depicts the level of political energy government authorities were willing to exert to curtail what seemed to them to be a political and religious threat to the *pax romanum* and *pax deorum.*[14] The importance and use of the *Acts* by the early church expresses this precarious socio-political situation. Uncertain of a peaceful co-existence with their pagan counterparts, the church looked to its scriptures and to the witness of the martyrs and their visions for strength and encouragement. The role of the *Acts* in honoring the anniversary of the martyr's death and, particularly, her/his *re-birth* and entry into the heavenly realms is one example of how the persecuted church used them to build their strength and be encouraged.[15] All or portions of the *Acts* were read or incorporated into a sermon on the day of the anniversaries of the martyr(s)'s rebirth, and a eucharist was celebrated, usually at the gravesite(s) where the martyr(s) was buried.[16] The earliest mention of the purpose and practice of this celebration is found in the second century document, the Martyrdom of Polycarp:[17]

> And so, when the centurion noticed the conflict caused by the Jews, he put the body [of Polycarp] out before everyone and had it cremated, as is their [i.e. pagan] custom. Thus, at last, collecting the remains that were dearer to us than precious stones and finer than gold, we buried them in a fitting spot. Gathering here, so far as we can, in joy and gladness, we will be allowed by the Lord to celebrate the birthday[18] of his martyrdom, both as a memorial for those who have already fought the contest and for the training and preparation of those who will do so one day.[19]

By the third century, the practice of the celebration of the anniversary of the martyrs had spread throughout the churches in the Roman empire. It had also expanded to include the commemoration of those Christians who died as a result of being "in prison and in bonds" for the sake of their faith. For instance, during the Decian persecution (250-251) Cyprian, Bishop of Carthage, writes to his presbyters and deacons admonishing them to:

> Mark the days on which they [those who died in prison] depart, that we may celebrate their memories among the commemorations of the martyrs:...Tertullus,...hath written and still writes, and acquaints me [Cyprian] with the days on which our blessed brethren in prison pass by the way of a glorious death to immortality; and oblations and sacrifices in commemoration of them are here celebrated by us, which, the Lord protecting, we shall soon celebrate with you.[20]

According to Cyprian, those who died while in prison were also to be counted among the martyrs.[21]

The reading of these *Acts* also allowed for a continual (re)hearing of the visions. The belief that the martyr's visions were prophetic--meant to address the church universal--would have further allowed the believer to re-envision and thus also re-appropriate the vision(s) and what they promised, for her/himself. As a result, visions would have been continually re-birthed and re-cast in the hearer's mind to reflect the new protagonist, i.e. the hearer, and her or his particular situation. This was possible because of the visions' universal theme, particularly its underlying witness of the promise of victory in martyrdom (or persecution) and an eternal recompense with God. This brings us to another of the church's use of the *Acts* and the visions, mainly, their role in strengthening the churches that were left without their spiritual leaders.

In persecutions that aggressively targeted the leaders of the church (e.g. those initiated by the emperors Maximinus the Thracian, and Valerian), Christians suffered the loss of their bishop(s), presbyters and deacons. The impact of their grief is particularly expressed in the Martyrdom of Fructuosus and Companions.[22] Fructuosus was the first bishop of Tarragona, a Roman province that according to tradition was evangelized by St. Paul.[23] Fructuosus was martyred in 259 with his two deacons, Augurius and Eulogius. Their loss caused the church to feel abandoned. The narrator writes:

> But the Christians [*fratres*] were sad, as those who are abandoned without a shepherd and burdened with sorrow, and this not because they felt sorrow for

Fructuosus, but rather because they missed him and recalled the memory of the faith and the contest of each of the martyrs.[24]

The *Acts* helped to strengthen the mournful Tarragonan Christians through exhortation and stories about experiences of divine visions and miracles. The sadness of the bishopless church of Tarragona was eclipsed by the miracles that apparently took place after church members collected the ashes of the martyrs and "claimed them for their own." The narrator explains how these "miracles of our Lord and Saviour were not wanting to increase the faith of believers and to set an example to the young."[25] He reminded the church that the martyrdom of Fructuosus was necessary to:

> confirm in his own bodily suffering and resurrection that which he had by God's mercy in our Lord and Saviour, when he was alive and teaching in the world.[26]

The bishop's "resurrection," and subsequently that of the deacons', are confirmed through a vision wherein Fructuosus "together with his deacons in robes of glory" appeared to certain parishioners and to Aemilianus who had condemned him to death.[27] After this visionary event, the narrator writes that Christians were filled with "great fear and joy."[28] The church was edified and reminded that the death of the martyrs was to be seen, not as a defeat for the churches left without their beloved bishop, but as another triumph over the Devil. Thus the narrator exclaims:

> Ah, blessed martyrs, who were tested in the fire like precious gold, clad in the breastplate of faith and the helmet of salvation, crowned with a diadem and a *crown that does not fade* because they trod underfoot the Devil's head! Ah, blessed martyrs, who earned a worthy dwelling-place in heaven, standing at the right hand of Christ, blessing God the almighty Father, Jesus Christ his son, and the Holy Spirit! Amen.[29]

If anything, the martyr's new place "at the right hand of Christ" was to be understood as a cause for the church to rejoice.

Through the Martyrdom of Fructuosus and Companions one can see that visions, like the Acts, had a significant role in the edification of the church. In the prologue of the Martyrdom of Perpetua and Felicitas, the author further describes the role of visions in the life of the believer as one of "blessing":

> So we too hold in honour and acknowledge not only new prophecies but new visions as well, according to the promise [Acts 2:17-18, Joel 2:28]. And we consider all other functions of the Holy Spirit as intended for the good of the Church; for the same Spirit has been sent to distribute all his gifts to all, as the Lord apportions to everyone....Thus no one of weak or despairing faith may think that supernatural grace was present only among men of ancient times, either in the grace of martyrdom or of *visions*, for God always achieves what he promises, as a witness to the non-believer and a blessing to the faithful.[30]

The special "grace of [new] visions" is understood here to be as equally dynamic in the third century church as in the "men of ancient times." New visions were held "in honour and acknowledged" as a promise of God for the continued building up (i.e. blessing, benefit) of the church. This is especially depicted in the Martyrdom of Montanus and Lucius. Renus, one of the martyrs, has a vision wherein he sees himself and the other Christians imprisoned with him being brought forth to execution:

> As each of us advanced one by one, a lamp was carried in front of him. No one went forward without a lamp going ahead of him. And after he had seen us pass by with our lamps he awoke. And we were glad when he told us the story, believing that we were walking with Christ, who is a *lamp unto our feet*, and indeed the Word of God.[31]

Renus' vision of them being led by the lamp, or as is interpreted by the writer, by Christ "who is a lamp unto our feet," gave them a new insight into their predicament that caused them to be glad. In their painful path to martyrdom, not one of them would go forward "without Christ (i.e. the lamp) going before them" leading the way. And, so the narrator continues, "After that night we spent a very happy day."[32]

Visions were also thought to function as "a witness to the non-believer." This "witness" sometimes went beyond the written page. In the Martyrdom of Potamiaena and Basilides, for instance, Basilides, a pagan soldier who had led Potamiaena to her execution, is said to have made a "strange and sudden turn" to Christianity.[33] When asked why, Basilides replied that Potamiaena had appeared[34] to him three days after her martyrdom and "put a crown on his head; she said that she had requested his grace from the Lord and had obtained her prayer, and that she would welcome him before long."[35] For Basilides, the apparition (promised him by Potamiaena before her execution) functioned as a powerful witness to the truth of the faith of Potamiaena inspiring him to endure his own execution.

But the *Acts* also played a major role in "preparing" the martyr for the "contest"--the possible martyrdom. Should the Christian's strength wane she or he had only to attend to page after page of stories testifying to the witness of martyrs of all ages and social and ecclesial ranks who "glorifying God,...fulfilled their testimony by their act of faith."[36] If this was not enough, the martyrs' own words could be found exhorting the Christian to, for instance:

> hasten with all eagerness, with as much courage as you can, that it may be given to you to see the Lord, and that he may reward you with a similar crown.[37]

The role of the *Acts* in preparing the martyr was further enhanced by visions' vivid portrayal of the martyrs' spiritual and physical struggles and of their eternal rewards. The vision of Perpetua illustrates this well. The day before she was to fight the beasts, she experiences a vision where she is attacked by an "Egyptian...of vicious appearance"[38]:

> We [Perpetua and her opponent] drew close to one another and began to let our fists fly. My opponent tried to get hold of my feet, but I kept striking him in the face with the heels of my feet...I put my two hands together linking the fingers of one hand with those of the other and thus I got hold of his head. He fell flat on his face and I stepped on his head. The crowd began to shout and my assistants started to sing psalms. Then I walked up to the trainer and took the branch. He kissed me and said to me: 'Peace be with you, my daughter!' I began to walk in triumph towards the Gate of Life.[39]

In her vision, Perpetua was fighting a spiritual battle. The physical contest she would have to endure the next day in the Roman arena is transposed in the vision into a metaphor for the *real* battle--with the Devil! Thus, she writes, "Then I awoke. I realized that it was not with wild animals that I would fight but with the Devil, but I knew that I would win the victory."[40] Perpetua's visionary knowledge of her pending victory helped prepare her for the struggle awaiting her in the arena.

In the Martyrdom of Montanus and Lucius, Flavian, a deacon, experiences a vision that also prepared him for the trials of martyrdom. Flavian has been preoccupied with his fear of pain and suffering. His vision, which he dictates to a fellow Christian, addresses this:

> 'In the days when our Bishop Cyprian was our only martyr,' he [Flavian] said, 'this was the vision I had. I thought I asked Cyprian whether the final death blow was painful, for as martyr-to-be I wished to ask his advice on bearing the pain. 'His reply to me was: "It is another flesh that suffers when the soul is in heaven. The body does not feel this at all when the mind is entirely absorbed in God."'[41]

Flavian's (and through him other martyrs') fear of pain is addressed; "it is another flesh that suffers when the soul is in heaven." Further, the martyr receives instruction to keep his mind "entirely absorbed in God." The insinuation here is that the mind that is stayed on God will not be occupied with thoughts of pain and suffering. This sort of 'mind over body' exercise would insure that "the body does not feel [pain] at all." At this point the narrator shares his own excitement for what he has just heard:

> What an exchange, with one martyr encouraging the other! The one denied the final death-blow hurt in order that the other, who was yet about to die, might be filled with more courage since he would not fear the slightest sense of pain in the final blow.[42]

Although the narrator's use of the word "*denied*" (*negauit*) reveals his sense of disbelief in a completely painless martyrdom, both the martyr and the narrator seem encouraged by this vision. Thus, at his martyrdom, Flavian is said to have stood valiantly amidst his fellow Christians encouraging and admonishing them to "love one another as I (Christ) have loved you." Then, after a "most abundant eulogy" destining the priest Lucian for the bishopric,[43] he knelt down "as though to pray" completing his martyrdom with a prayer.[44]

Finally, visions functioned as mirrors into the whereabouts and status of the martyr.

> Ah, how great and glorious is God's favour to his dear ones! Oh, the genuine, fatherly kindness of Jesus Christ our Lord, who shows such great benefits to his beloved and so reveals himself before bestowing the gifts of his mercy....Marian and James and the rest of the clergy were at last restored to the patriarchs in glory and were delivered from the distress of this world.[45]

The "great benefits" expressed here refers to the gift of visions by which the Lord "reveals himself before bestowing the gifts of his mercy." The author has complete confidence that the martyrs are now at the place revealed to them by the vision(s), that is, with the "patriarchs in glory."

The role of the Acts in honoring the memory and re-birth of the martyrs, and their function in the edification and preparation of the Christian for possible martyrdom also influenced the role and function of the visions of the martyrs contained therein. The visions of the martyrs were a vivid reminder of the martyr's re-birth and entry into the heavenly abode. The favor of "God's benefits" through visions also served as a visionary epiphany of God's presence, reminding the believer that in the midst of trials, they were not alone. With the *Acts,* visions also functioned as a divine witness to believers and non-believers. As noted above, the conversion of the Roman soldier Basilides was influenced by his vision of Potamiaena. The divinely inspired depictions of pending victory and eternal glory awaiting the martyr also helped to strengthen the believer for his/her own "contest." Visions facilitated the process of martyrdom by addressing the martyrs' fears and instructing them to, for instance, be "absorbed in God."

Christians in the Roman empire, and beyond, read the Acts and the *passiones* and found solace in the message of hope and the visions of glory that would, one day, also be their inheritance.

# Conclusion

The early church believed there was an intricate relationship between the function of the Acts of the Martyrs and the visions depicted in many of its pages. Each served to inform and enrich the other: the one providing the details of the last events leading toward the martyrdom, and the other providing divinely revealed vistas of the martyrs' victorious end and heavenly destination. Together they worked coactively providing the reader with a more complete picture of what it meant, and was like, to suffer and die for the sake of their Christ. Issues of fear concerning physical pain, length of torture, or the possibility of apostatizing; of sorrow for loved ones that would be left behind (e.g. Perpetua and Felicitas for their newborn babies, bishops for their parishoners); as well as issues regarding the certainty of future life with God and the saints, are only fully grasped when both the Acts and the visions are resourced. In addition, this synergic relationship informed and assured the reader of the dynamic presence of divine activity fortifying and enlightning the martyr's steps toward the arena.

To understand the reciprocally reinforcing relationship between the Acts and the visions is to begin to understand the degree of force they exerted against the prevailing socio-political situation of the times. It has already been established that the Acts were widely distributed and read throughout the empire and beyond. This popularity was enhanced by several literary factors that worked in favor of the martyrs and the church. Among these was their simple style and language.

The Acts were written by church folk for church folk. The threatening socio-political situations the church faced left little time for embarking on deep theological and/or philosophical excursions. The universal theme framing the Acts was direct and simple: it was a testimony and a witness to the promise of victory in martyrdom and, particularly through the visions, the sure recompense of eternal bliss with God. This also applied to the visions--that new and or different way of seeing that did not rely on rational analysis or formularies. Through the visions, the martyr saw and believed s/he had experienced a preview of the rewards of her/his greater hope. The martyr saw and smelled the flora that adorned paradise; heard the singing of the trees praising their creator; kissed their Lord, and savored the sweetness of eternal life in the promised land.[46] This sensorial appeal made the visions aesthetically attractive and invigorating. It also made them all the more credible and thus dangerous to Roman ends.

The brevity of the Acts (and the visions) likely also contributed to their popularity and power. Most Acts were but a few pages long. This meant that they could easily have been memorized and shared orally, and/or copied, translated and clandestinely disseminated. These literary factors, including the visions' power to evoke the senses and give an impression of an actual experience, functioned as critical weapons in the church's spiritual warfare against the forces of the Roman empire.

Important also was the fact that the stories of the martyrdoms and the visions were closer to the times and circumstances of the second to fourth century church than the stories of the martyrs (and their visions) in the Hebrew and Christian scriptures. This contemporary witness would have also contributed to their popularity and to their ability to move the reader, who may have personally known the martyr.

Finally, the Acts, together with the visions contained within, provided a sobering, yet hopeful testimony. Death would be met with life and suffering with unending joy. This testimony became a literary and spiritual tool against the state's attempt to bend the believer's resolve. It was a subversive tool that proclaimed that Christ only, not the emperor nor life in the great Roman empire, was worth living and even dying for.

Through visions the eschatological kingdom of God became immediate. One of the effects of this experience of immediacy was its ability to influence the transposition of one reality for another believed to be more gratifying.[47] The power of visions to influence the martyr is exemplified in the next chapter with the vision of Saturus in the Martyrdom of Perpetua and Felicitas and the vision of Polycarp. This chapter will especially show how visions undermined not only the political state, but theological and social norms as well.

## Notes

1. Gary A. Bisbee distinguishes between *acts Christianorum* (the acts of the Christian martyrs) and *acta martyrum* (acts of either pagan or Christian martyrs). Since our concentration on Christian martyrs does not necessitate such distinctions, we will refer to this kind of literature as the Acts of the Martyrs or Acts. *Pre-Decian Acts of Martyrs and Commentarii* (Philadelphia: Fortress, 1988) 4.

2. Those who exclude the *Acts of Ignatius* as inauthentic begin the origin and development of the genre in the mid-second century with the *Martyrdom of Polycarp* (died betw. 155-177) and the *Martyrdom of Ptolemaeus and Lucius* (died before 160).

Bisbee, however, advocates for the inclusion of the *Acts of Ignatius* in the discussion on the origin and development of the genre. See Bisbee 4,5, 85-85.

3. Bisbee 5 and 83. See also Bueno 137. The belief that the *Acts* emerged from official court discourses is based on the alleged authenticity of these documents. This belief has been put to the test by Gary A. Bisbee. In his book, *Pre-Decian Acts of Martyrs and Commentarii*, he shows that many of these (and consequently the ensuing) *Acts* did not entirely conform (some not at all) to *commentarius*-form. Consequently, the criteria used to determine authenticity is quixotic since many of these documents have undergone revision. Authenticity, he argues, must necessarily be a measurement of "the degree of editorial revision thought or known to be present" in the document. This distinction is important for it shows the problem inherent in the process of selecting and classifying, in our case, visions into "authentic" or "inauthentic" categories (83-84). For an in-depth analysis of this genre see Bisbee's work.

4. (My translation). See Victor Saxer, "Afrique latine" in *Corpus Christianorum: Hagiographies* (Brepols, 1994) 1: 33. *La simplicité de leur rédaction avait sans doute autant de force persuasive qu'un éloquent panégyrique.*

5. Saxer 86.

6. W. H. C. Frend, *Martyrdom and Persecution in the Early Church: A Study of a Conflict from the Maccabees to Donatus* (Oxford: Basil, 1965) xi.

7. Martyrologies, not to be confused with the *passiones*, were used as official registers of the martyrs' death. The earliest took the form of calendars recording the martyrs name and the place of martyrdom under the day of her/his anniversary.

8. Frend xi.

9. Daniel Ruíz Bueno has a detailed and interesting essay regarding the Acts of the Martyrs. *Actas de los Mártires* Texto Bilingue (Madrid: Editorial Católica, 1968) 136-149.

10. Canon 13 states: *De his qui Scripturas sanctas tradidisse dicuntur vel vasa dominica vel nomina fratrum suorum, placuit nobis ut quicumque eorum ex actis ublicis fuerit detectus, non nudis verbis, ab ordine cleri amoveantur.* In Ruíz Bueno 138.

11. See Bisbee 122, n. 15 and especially Musurillo lviii-lxii.

12. Bisbee 122.

13. Musurillo 313, ch. 2.19.

14. Bisbee 122 and Musurillo lxii.

15. Or *dies natalis*.

16. With the development of the cult of the relics, the celebration was, by mid third century, moved into the church where their remains were buried. In the Martyrdom of Fructuosus and Companions (259), for example, we are told that their remains were buried "in the holy church under the holy altar." See Musurillo 185, nt. 15 which cites the version in the manuscripts used by P. Franchi de'Cavalieri. For more information on this version see also xxxii.

17. Scholars have not been able to agree on the exact date of Polycarp's martyrdom. However, the traditional accepted date is Feb. 155 or 156. Musurillo xiii.

18. Musurillo uses "anniversary" for *genéthlion* but I think "birthday" might better capture the theology behind the early church practice.

19. Musurillo 17, ch. 18.

20. Cyprian's Epistle 12.2 in *The Epistles of S. Cyprian, Bishop of Carthage and Martyr, with The Council of Heretics,* trans. Members of the English Church (Oxford: Parker, 1844)30.

21. For more information on who was a martyr, see chapter one.

22. Musurillo 172-185.

23. Tarragona was also the first province to erect a temple to Augustus. Ruíz Bueno 783.

24. Ruíz Bueno 183, ch. 6.1. According to Musurillo, chapters 5-7 of the Martyrdom of Fructuosus and Companions, which tell of the bishop's appearances after his death, and the eulogistic ending might have been written later by a "more pious hand." He also states, however, that the "the *acta* surely existed before 400." The fact that Augustine and Prudentius know of the *acta* supports this conclusion. The possibility that chs. 5-7 may have been a later addition does not subtract from the role of the *Acts* and visions in strengthening and encouraging the church. If chs. 5-7 were added by the editor, he did so in acknowledgment of the importance of the role and function the *Acts* and the visions played in the community.

25. Musurillo 183, ch. 6.2.
26. Musurillo 183, ch. 6.3.
27. Musurillo 185, ch. 7.1.
28. Musurillo 185, n. 15. This is found in the manuscripts cited by P. Franchi de' Cavalieri. See Musurillo xxxii for more information.
29. Musurillo 185, ch. 7.2 (italics in Musurillo).
30. Musurillo 107, ch. 1:5.
31. Musurillo 217, ch. 5.1-2.
32. Musurillo 219, ch. 6.1
33. Musurillo 135.
34. Visions also usually included special apparitions. Among the most revered apparitions is the figure of the Shepherd who exhorts and encourages the martyr to do battle against her/his persecutors usually personified as Satan or the Anti-Christ, another common figure. It was neither unusual nor uncommon for martyrs to have visions in which other martyrs, usually family members or key members of their church community who had gone before them, appeared offering them words of hope and encouragement.

Differences between a revelation, vision, and an apparition are inconsequential to this study. In his work, David E. Aune shows the futility in distinguishing among different types of visions, especially as these "refinements often contribute little to understanding or defining the genre." (*Prophecy* 99. See also p. 373, . 147 of his book).

35. Musurillo 135, ch. 6.
36. From the "Martyrdom of Saints Justin, Chariton, Charito, Evelpistus, Hierax, Paeon, Liberian, and their Community," Musurillo 47, ch. 6.
37. From the "Acts of Maximilian," Musurillo 249, ch. 3.2.
38. Musurillo 119, ch. 10.6.
39. Musurillo 119, ch.10.10-13.
40. Musurillo 119, ch. 10.14.
41. Musurillo 235, ch. 21.3-4. The quotation marks reflect those within Musurillo's translation.
42. Musurillo 235, ch. 21.5.
43. Musurillo 239, ch. 23.4.
44. Musurillo 239, ch. 23.6.
45. Musurillo 239, ch. 11.7-8.
46. This is particularly so in the vision of Saturus in the "Martyrdom of Perpetua and Felicitas." More is said of this vision in chs. 4 and 5 of this book.
47. Not all martyrs had visions. However, this did not prevent a martyr (or any other Christian) from appropriating a martyr's vision for her/himself. This is especially true since visions were believed to be prophetic. Further, I do not want to minimize the role of faith. Faith in the promise and immediacy of the kingdom revealed allowed for the ability to transpose one reality for another.

# Chapter 4

# Death and the "Hour of Triumph": Subversion within the Visions of Saturus and Polycarp

I alluded in the beginning of this book to the rich metaphorical and symbolical content of the visions of the martyrs. It is my contention that the *symbols*, *images*, *metaphors*, and *signs* inherent within the visions were interpreted subversively against the prevailing oppressive contexts.[1] But, who would have understood these signs? What are the religious and or cultural codes that would help the reader unlock the meaning(s) referenced by these signs and thus arrive at their subversive nature?[2] An analysis of the visions of Saturus (Martyrdom of Perpetua and Felicitas) and of bishop Polycarp of Smyrna illustrate how these questions can be answered. Both of these visions provide a succinct example of the role of images, metaphors, and signs in evoking meaning--beyond the stated obvious and against prevailing norms.

## The Vision of Saturus in the Passion of Perpetua and Felicitas

" A number of young catechumens were arrested...."[3] Thus begins the account of the martyrdom of Perpetua, Felicitas, Saturus their teacher, and others, thought to have been compiled soon after their deaths in the year 203 CE. On the eve of his martyrdom, Saturus had a vision. "We [he and Perpetua, a 22 year old mother of an infant son] had died, he said, and had put off the flesh."[4] Then they were "carried towards the east by four angels."[5] Upon entering what he described to be a beautiful garden, they were paid homage by four angels "more splendid than the others"[6] who, judging by their excitement, were anxiously awaiting the martyrs' arrival. Saturus vividly goes on to describe their experience before the throne of God,[7] and the meeting of the elders who gave them the "kiss of peace" and bid them "Go and play."[8] As Saturus and Perpetua went before the gates they had an interesting encounter:

> Then we went out and before the gates we saw the bishop Optatus on the right and Aspasius the presbyter and teacher on the left, each of them far apart and in sorrow. They threw themselves at our feet and said: 'Make peace between us. For you have gone away and left us thus.' And we said to them: 'Are you not our bishop, and are you not our presbyter? How can you fall at our feet?'[9]

It turns out that the bishop and his presbyter had been quarreling between themselves and were still in discord. Their disagreement apparently accounts for their being outside or "before the gates" rather than inside the gates as Perpetua and Saturus had been. Much to Saturus' amazement, both the bishop Optatus and the presbyter Aspasius throw themselves at his and his catechumen's feet and plea for their succor, for "it seemed that they [the angels] wanted to close the gates."[10] Saturus' and Perpetua's questions "Are you not our bishop, and are you not our presbyter? How can you fall at our feet?," are revealing. They not only point to the ecclesiastical codes that dictated the norm--bishops and presbyters do not kneel before their parishioners and, much less, ask for their mediation--they indicate that what has happened is a complete reversal of those codes. Even more striking is the fact that, according to the vision, this reversal took place within the heavenly garden, thus setting the anomaly within the context of divine approval.

The implications of this vision become clear when explored against its particular historical-theological settings. By the third century, the time of Saturus and Perpetua's martyrdom, there had already developed a gender-exclusive ecclesiastical hierarchy of which the apex was the bishop followed by the presbyter and deacons. Finally, comprising the floor of the pyramid were the catechumens and the hearers. In his *Letter to the Magnesians* (c.107) Ignatius, bishop of Antioch in Syria, assumes this order:

> Let the bishop preside in God's place, and the presbyters take the place of the apostolic council, and let the deacons (my special favorites) be entrusted with the ministry of Jesus Christ who was with the Father from eternity and appeared at the end [of the world].[11]

Writing to the church at Ephesus, Ignatius also exhorted them to "regard the bishop as the Lord himself"[12] and to "heed the bishop and presbytery attentively."[13] Saturus' question to bishop Optatus and Aspasius the presbyter leads us to believe that Saturus may not have been a presbyter as has been previously assumed.[14] Herbert Musurillo, for instance, goes as far as saying that he was a "young catechumen."[15] Other scholars, however, refer to Saturus as a catechist or teacher.[16] Unfortunately, the textual evidence can be used to support either of the latter two conclusions. For instance, we recall that Severus' edict of 202 was aimed at new converts and proselytizers. In this light, Perpetua's statement that Saturus had later given himself up of his own accord because "he was not present when we were arrested," can mean either of two things. First, that had Saturus, himself a catechumen, been present among the others, he would also have been arrested. On the other hand, as their catechist, it could mean that Saturus would have been arrested for proselytizing. Either way, it seems to imply that Saturus felt some sense of commitment to, or bond with, his fellow catechumens or students (whatever the case) that compelled him to give himself up and accompany them to their martyrdom. Second, Perpetua's mention of Saturus as the "builder of our strength," might be used to support the argument for his role as teacher.[17] However, Perpetua herself is portrayed as building the faith of the other catechumens.[18] Finally, reference to other Christians within the Passio seem always to include their ecclesial (or social) standing. This pattern continues throughout the text. For instance, Tertius and Pomponius, (not imprisoned) are identified as "deacons," Optatus as "the bishop" and Aspasius as "the presbyter."[19] Saturus, on the other hand, is not called by any ecclesiastical title.

The most that can be assumed regarding Saturus is that he was a lay person who was also possibly a catechist.[20] He was definitely not a presbyter. Further, Saturus' question to the presbyter Aspasius and bishop Optatus makes more sense within the context of a lay person. For Saturus, the higher ranking bishop and presbyter's act of humbling themselves before two 'little' ones is puzzling and alarming. (Thus he, with Perpetua,[21] exclaims, "Aren't you our father and you our priest? How then do you throw yourselves at our feet?"). In the vision of this simple teacher the ecclesiastical pyramid which, according to St. Ignatius reflected the celestial economy, is inverted. The earthly ecclesiastical order is subverted by the divine disorder where 'the last shall be first' and 'the humble shall sit with princesses.'[22]

The theological and ecclesial impact of this vision's subversive dimension is perhaps best illustrated by the controversy which arose after the

Decian persecution fifty years later.[23] The Carthaginian confessors' act of restoring the lapsed to the communion of the church resonates with the vision's depiction of the inverted pyramid—where bishop and presbyter kneel at the feet of the two martyrs. Popular view held that a martyr's death held atoning virtue for others. In one of his many letters to the martyrs, Cyprian, the bishop of Carthage, affirmed this popular view. According to Cyprian the prayers of the martyrs were more efficacious than his own:

> For since your voice [the martyr's] is clearly more efficacious in petition and your prayers in afflictions more easily obtain what they seek, pray and ask more eagerly, that the divine grace may consummate the confession of all of us, that God may also free us together with you undefiled and glorious from the darkness and the snares of the world.[24]

In North Africa the "powers of forgiveness universally ascribed to them [the martyrs], raised their status beyond that of the clergy."[25] The following request from the confessor Celerinus to his fellow-confessor Lucianus regarding absolution for two women who had committed the sin of apostasy supports this claim:

> I pray, my lord, and beseech you, through Our Lord Jesus Christ, to inform and to ask your associates, your brethren, my lords, that whoever of you shall first

receive the crown, grant forgiveness for their grave sin (of apostasy) to our sisters Numeria and Candida.[26]

According to Cyprian, however, only the bishop possessed the authority to reconcile an apostate to the church. "Let them (the priests)," he tells the confessors and martyrs, "reserve your petitions and desires for the *bishop* and await a peaceful and suitable time for granting your requests."[27] For Cyprian, the act of forgiving the lapsed outside of ecclesiastical authority was scandalous--it was a subversion of the laws of God, an usurpation of the authority of the bishop and, in the end, endangered the unity of the church. His struggle to maintain and solidify, what was, in his view, the "right order in the Church"[28] against the popular view that elevated the status and authority of the martyrs above that of the bishop is reflected in several of his Epistles:

> The responsibility of our position and our fear of the Lord compels us, most brave and most blessed martyrs to admonish you by our letter that those by whom the faith of the Lord is so devotedly kept, should likewise observe the law and discipline of the Lord. For it is the duty of all of the soldiers of Christ to obey the commands of their supreme commander, then it becomes you still more to be obedient to His orders, you who have become an example to others, both of valor and of the fear of God.[29]

In his letter to a number of apostates who were seeking reconciliation with the church based on letters of recommendation written on their behalf by the martyr Paulus, Cyprian further insists upon episcopal authority in all matters:

> Our Lord, whose precepts we ought to revere and to observe, providing for the honor of the bishop and the order of His Church, speaks in the Gospel and says to Peter: 'I say unto you that thou art Peter and upon this rock I shall build my Church, and the gates of hell shall not conquer it, and to thee I shall give the keys of the kingdom of heaven, and whatsoever thou shalt bind on earth shall also be bound in heaven, and whatsoever thou shalt loose on earth shall also be loosed in heaven' (Matt. 16, 18f.). According to this, through the changes of the times and the succession in office, the appointment of bishops and the right order in the Church is founded on the bishops and *every act of the Church is governed by these same prelates.*[30]

Saturus' vision, on the other hand, affirms the peculiar status and intercessory authority of the martyrs. Given the *Passio*'s wide-spread popularity, it is very likely that it helped to further solidify this popular view among the laity and the confessors. In any case, the result is that the confessors were going over and above the bishop (i.e. Cyprian) and, by their own merits, were receiving back the penitent lapsed into the church. Cyprian's efforts and future councils would later legislate against this practice.

When the person of Perpetua is, even briefly, considered, we realize that the ramifications of this vision extend well beyond the ecclesiastical context. Perpetua's role as martyr-prophet and intercessor suggest the existence of an alternative theological code that transcended ecclesiastical boundaries. We recall that Perpetua was not only a mere catechumen, she was also a woman and mother. Studies show that by the beginning of the second century, the church had begun to espouse and promote the dominant patriarchal values shared by

Jews and Gentiles.³¹ By this time, women's social and religious roles were relegated and intricately tied to procreation and motherhood. However, glimpses of this eschatological vision of equality were preserved in the Christian Scriptures and other writings such as the *Apocryphal Acts* and, as we have seen, in the *Acts of the Martyrs* which "held a central place in doctrine and devotion."³² Against this theological and social backdrop, Saturus' vision of the bishop and presbyter kneeling at this young mother's feet not only implies an inversion of the ecclesiastical pyramid--it poignantly suggests a reversal of the social codes that dictated the norm. To those around her, Perpetua was not primarily a mother; she was foremost "a valiant and blessed martyr....called and chosen for the glory of Christ Jesus."³³

Finally, from Saturus' vision it is possible to surmise that visions probably became powerful carriers of an existential newness characterized by a "kin-dom" that was present and yet still to come.³⁴ As carriers of this newness, visions helped the reader transcend present circumstances by compelling the Christian to envision and live out of that new interstitial domain manifested in her/his hope of what is and is yet to be.³⁵ Saturus' vision lends itself to the sort of cultural analysis characteristic of Homi K. Bhabha. In his book, The Location of Culture, Bhabha describes the world of alternative possibilities wrought by the interruption of cultural interstices that question, for example, past and present binary divisions. The result is an "unhomely" condition that negates "the time-barrier of a culturally collusive 'present'."³⁶ To be "unhomely" is not, as he describes, to be homeless. Rather, it is to exist within the emergent boundary, "the bridge where 'presencing' begins."³⁷ Thus, the unhomely dwells beyond the binary division (e.g. of public and private spheres) in that other in-between space that both bridges and redefines current social boundaries. Bhabha's argument, though descriptive of those who live "'otherwise' than modernity but not outside it"³⁸ resonates well with the role of visions in evoking an existence within and yet beyond the martyr's 'present.' The martyr's unhomely condition is preempted by Jesus' teaching that his followers are in this world but are not of the world.³⁹ It is initiated by the seer's act of living out of that existential in-betweeness portrayed by the visions and characterized by her/his belief in a realized, yet eschatological kin-dom.

This dynamic ability of the martyr to exist between present-future horizons, in turn, defied all boundaries of time and space, life and death, powers and principalities. The result is a subaltern existence that is uniquely subversive. Saturus' awakening response to the vision of his new life within the heavenly garden provides a pithy example of the visions' power to evoke this subaltern existence:

> And there [in the heavenly garden] we began to recognize many of our brethren, martyrs among them. All of us were sustained by a most delicious odour that seemed to satisfy us. *And then I woke up happy.*⁴⁰

The state of being happy amidst oppressive conditions and impending death clearly subverts the state's attempts at crippling the Christian's resolve to remain faithful. The vision of the believer's promised future with God becomes, through the seer/recorder or reader's appropriation of it, the present that is and yet is not.

In his vision, the future breaks into Saturus' present compelling him to enter into that new interstitial domain where happiness is not a mere chimera but a genuine possibility.[41] From the margins of persecution, there emerges a new understanding of existence that overpowers, indeed relativizes, the notion of earthly (pagan) life as the center of what it means to be. It is also from the recesses of this periphery that the contours of time and space become extended--beyond the third century and the Roman empire--to include eternity with God in a universe without oppressive borders. From this subaltern existence the seer, in this case, Saturus, (but also Perpetua and the others) becomes empowered to stand and overcome even the cruelest of deaths.

Polycarp, the 86 year-old bishop of Smyrna, also experienced a vision before his death. The account of his martyrdom written in the form of a letter to the church of Philomelium and to "all the holy Catholic Church" has remained popular throughout time.[42] Every now and then, from any corner of the world, one can still hear Polycarp's famous words passionately resounding from our churches' pulpits: "For eighty-six years I have been his servant and he has done me no wrong. How can I blaspheme against my king and saviour?"[43] Unfortunately, the depth and power hidden within Polycarp's vision have, for the most part, remained unexplored and therefore, untapped. I turn now to his vision.

## The Vision of Polycarp

Early in the second century, the frail and aged Polycarp, Bishop of Smyrna, stood in the amphitheater before a tumultuous crowd and the proconsul. He had been arrested at the irate cry of an angry mob for being, in their view, "the schoolmaster of Asia--the father of the Christians--the destroyer of our gods--the one that teaches the multitude not to sacrifice or do reverence!"[44] "Three days before his arrest," while at prayer, "he had a vision and saw his pillow blazing[45] with fire, and turning to those who were with him he said, 'I must be burned alive.'"[46] The proconsul's failed attempt at sparing his life by persuading Polycarp to "have respect to your age,".... "curse Christ" and "swear by the fortune of Caesar" outraged the crowd who then requested he be burned alive.[47] "For the vision he [Polycarp] had seen regarding his pillow," the narrator writes, "had to be fulfilled."[48]

The vision of the blazing pillow had several functions. The first and most obvious one is explicitly given to us in the interpretation, " I must be burned alive." The image of the blazing pillow functioned as a sign of his proximate death by fire. One might even say that the blazing pillow became an icon for death and a metaphor for the manner of death Polycarp would have to suffer.

But, might there be more to this vision that is not directly expressed in his interpretation? For instance, Polycarp's statement that he would be burned alive considers only one part of the sign, that is, the image of the blazing fire. What about the image of the pillow? If the sole purpose of his vision was for him to know that he would be martyred by fire, then, why a blazing pillow and not a pile of blazing branches, for example? Why is there no direct reference to the meaning of the pillow itself? This leads us to believe that there may be a larger and perhaps even deeper meaning intended by the image of the blazing pillow. Further, that its meaning would possibly have been assumed by its readers. This assumed meaning becomes lucid through the process of literary analysis.

The juxtaposition of *blazing* with *pillow* is purposely puzzling for it clearly denotes a contradiction in terms. For instance, the noun *pillow* was associated with sleep and peaceful rest, with the setting of the sun and the dawn of a new day.[49] The adjective *blazing* or burning, on the other hand, implies fire which, when applied to the human body, is associated with horrible pain and possibly one's demise. A closer look at Polycarp's statements regarding his Christian beliefs will show that this contradiction in terms is only superficial. It will reveal that the burning pillow not only became for him an icon for death but also, and most importantly, for life--new, eternal life. This is not only implied but assumed throughout the text.[50] Polycarp's prayer supports this claim through its explicit reference to a new beginning through resurrection:

> *O Lord, omnipotent God* and Father of your beloved and blessed child Christ Jesus, through whom we have received our knowledge of you, the God of the angels, the powers, and of all creation, and of all the family of the good who live in your sight: I bless you because you have thought me worthy of this day and this hour, to have a share among the number of the martyrs in the cup of your Christ, *for the resurrection unto* eternal *life* of both the soul and the body in the immortality of the Holy Spirit. May I be received this day among them before your face as a rich and acceptable sacrifice, as you, the God of truth who cannot deceive, have prepared, revealed, and fulfilled before hand. Hence I praise you, I bless you, and I glorify you above all things, through that eternal and celestial high priest, Jesus Christ, your beloved child, through whom is glory to you with him and the Holy Spirit now and for all ages to come. Amen.[51]

One must admit that a prayer of such length points to a possible reconstruction of what only *may* have been Polycarp's prayer. Nevertheless, it clearly elucidates what was more than likely Polycarp and his community's understanding of death as but a necessary yet temporary means to resurrection unto a better life, that is, an eternal life with God. This belief is heard in the prayer's reference to "*the resurrection unto* eternal *life* of both the soul and the body in the immortality of the Holy Spirit."[52] It is also echoed in Polycarp's response to the governor's demand to "change his mind" and deny Christ. "The fire you threaten me with," Polycarp retorted, "burns *merely for a time* and is soon extinguished."[53]

Thus, the key to the meaning of the paradox of the blazing pillow lies within the prayer and the rest of the text. In them, we find the theological codes whose referent is a well established teleological understanding of life beyond death. This understanding was supported by Christianity's claim of Christ's own death and resurrection.

Polycarp's reference to the fire that "burns merely for a time," (i.e. versus "the fire of everlasting punishment and of judgment that is to come, which awaits the impious"[54]) opens the door to exploring anew his interpretation for the symbolic meaning of the word *blazing*. A fire that "burns merely for a time" implies a blazing, or in his case, a demise that is swift and expeditious. Hence,

Polycarp's emphasis on the expeditiousness of his death is signified by his interpretation of the menacing fire as burning "merely for a time." Further, his focus on the ephemeral nature of this fire eclipses any emphasis on the impending anguish produced by the burning of his flesh. This focus throws more light on the role and function of the pillow in his vision.

I have already alluded to the symbolic association between pillow and sleep and the dawn of a new day. Polycarp's expectation of a heavenly resurrection provides the teleological code that expresses an unequivocal connection between pillow and a temporary sleep. This connection allows the pillow in his vision to function as the key metaphorical link between things past and things new. Together, the words blazing and pillow signal a swift transition from a physical, even painful, death to a new heavenly existence. Thus, the presence of the word *pillow* not only softens the metaphor of a pillow blazing, it completes the meaning of the icon.

We must conclude that the opposition between burning and pillow powerfully underscores the temporality of Polycarp's suffering and the expectation of a reawakening of his "soul and body" into a new eternal day. Polycarp and his community's belief in the Christian's immortality after death, would make the step from the burning pillow to its function as an icon for swift death, and life, or new life with Christ, an easy and most natural one. Although not explicitly stated in the interpretation of his vision, Polycarp's hope of resurrection, as shown in the prayer and elsewhere within the text, turns the blazing pillow not only into a divine as well as metaphorical sign of his impending death by fire, it elevates it into an icon for the new life that awaited him, but after a short slumber.

The function of the vision of the burning pillow as an icon for the kind of death that signified a sleeping and reawakening into the dawn of eternal life with God, has subversive dimensions. Especially, as it pertains to second century Roman political power. While the state, deeming itself powerful and in control, purported to take Polycarp's life through fire, it in fact provided the means through which the martyr passed from one oppressive, and at times, painful life to the long awaited heavenly existence. Further, "to have a share among the number of the martyrs in the cup of...Christ," was, among others, considered a "blessed" and "noble" gift. Thus, for Polycarp and the Christian faithful, the vision of the blazing pillow upstaged and in fact subverted the power of the state to determine the Christian's fate. In addition, his vision was also instrumental in encouraging Polycarp (with others) in his faith, and in strengthening his resolve to die for it. For the Bishop and his community, the vision was not only a sign of his chosenness, but of God's presence with him. As it is written, this 86 year old Christian named Polycarp stood his ground before the powerful Roman empire and through his death overcame his oppressors.

## Conclusion

The formative and emerging church of the first four centuries thought of visions as a viable and authoritative medium for the revelation of God's will and purpose. Some of these visions are contained within the *Acts of the Martyrs*, a genre of literature that is thought to have begun circulating among the Christian communities in the 2nd century with the *Acts of Ignatius*. As shown above, the extensive and widespread use of the *Acts* among the third and fourth century Christians gives the historical-theologian ample reason to inquire into the content and function of the visions. Our short excursion through the visions of Polycarp and Saturus revealed theological, scriptual and socio-cultural nuances that defied their particular historical-theological contexts. I referred to these nuances or incongruences as the subversive dimensions of the visions of the martyrs.

In the vision of Saturus, for example, the bishop and presbyter's act of throwing themselves at the feet of the lay teacher and the female catechumen defied the already developed gender-exclusive ecclesiastical hierarchy. It also defied cultural codes that taught that women were inferior--biologically and culturally--to men. Even more striking is the fact that, according to the vision, the reversal of these ecclesiastical (and social) codes took place within God's heavenly garden, setting the anomaly within the context of divine approval. Saturus' vision thus helps us to see what may have been a reconstruction or re-viewing of the social and ecclesiastical power structures as conceived by the laity (e.g. Saturus). The confessors' act of restoring the lapsed to the communion of the church--outside of ecclesiastical authority--after the Decian persecution, is a vivid example of how that popular and subversive view was played out in daily life.

Visions also impacted the quality and the nature of earthly existence, especially in times of persecution. Their ability to evoke an interstitial-- here now yet still to come--domain subverted all earthly notions of time and space. For the seer/recorder or reader, the present "reality" was subverted by that new reality represented by the "otherwise" than-now-or-later visual interstice. In this subaltern existence--from this spatio-temporal margin--all other center's of thought and being are minimized, and their persuasive powers relativized.

In addition, the visions of Saturus and Polycarp helped us to re-affirm the existence and impact of a theology that professed life after death. This theology, as noted by the analysis of the vision of Polycarp, was so strong it was assumed by the seer/recorder or (Christian) reader. We also saw in the Martyrdom of Polycarp how a seemingly powerless vision--a blazing pillow--conveyed a powerful message of hope and resurrection. His vision overturned the state's belief and insistence on the primacy of earthly existence by proclaiming and graphically re-affirming the primacy of life in Christ. Polycarp's vision is especially important because it underscores the metaphorical and symbolical power of visions to evoke meaning beyond what is explicitly stated. This gives us all the more reason to consider the import of these visions upon the early church and upon our knowledge of it.

As shown, both visions provide us with a historical and theological basis for arguing on behalf of an underlying grass roots or popular theology that at times subverted the prescribed theological and, or socio-cultural norms.

Thus far we have explored only a portion of Saturus' vision. The next chapter takes up the rest of his vision focusing particularly on its liturgical references and deciphering its possible meanings through the use of Biblical intertextual analysis.

## Notes

1. Augustine, considered by many to be "the greatest semiotician of antiquity and the real founder of semiotics," defined sign as "a thing which, over and above the impression it makes on the senses, causes something else to come into the mind as a consequence of itself." Simply stated, a sign is everything that can be taken as something serving for something else." Or everything that, on the grounds of a previously established social [and ecclesial] convention can be taken as something standing for something else." Umberto Eco, *A Theory of Semiotics* (Bloomington: Indiana UP, 1979)16. For more information on Augustine's semiotic theory see Winfred Noth, *Handbook of Semiotics* (Indianapolis: Indiana UP, 1990)15.

2. Alex García-Rivera's book, *St Martín de Porres: The "little Stories" and the Semiotics of Culture*, has been very helpful in elucidating the role and use of semiotics, specifically in terms of culture. See especially pp. 36-39 (Maryknoll, New York: Orbis, 1995).

3. Musurillo 109, ch. 2.1.

4. Musurillo 119, ch. 11.2.

5. Musurillo 119, ch. 11.2.

6. Musurillo 121, ch. 11.7.

7. The vision does not say "God" but is unequivocal in its implication that the "aged man with white hair and a youthful face" before whom voices endlessly chanted "'Holy, holy, holy!'", was meant as God, or better still, the God-Christ. See p. 121, ch. 12 in Musurillo.

8. Musurillo 121, ch. 12.6.

9. Musurillo 121, ch. 13.1-3.

10. Musurillo 121, ch. 13.7.

11. In Richardson 95 (brackets in Richardson).

12. Richardson 89.

13. Richardson 93.

14. Frend, for example, refers to Saturus as a "Carthaginian priest." The "catechist Saturus," he continues, "was himself a presbyter." (363-364)

15. Musurillo xxvi. He makes no argument for his conclusion, however.

16. These include Ruíz Bueno 400; Cecil M. Robeck says that "it is quite possible that Saturus was the instructor of these new converts, although that position may also have been occupied by the teaching presbyter, Aspasius." See *Prophecy in Carthage: Perpetua, Tertullian, and Cyprian* (Cleveland: Pilgrim, 1992)70; Shewring says only that Saturus had been the means of the other martyrs' conversion. See *The Passion* xiv.

17. Musurillo 111, ch 4.5.

18. See for example, Musurillo 129, ch. 20.20.

19. Musurillo 109 and 121, chs. 2 and 13, respectively.

20. In the third century, this function was carried out by the lay, therefore implying that Saturus was among the laity who also functioned as a catechist.

21. Frend puts the questions to the bishop and presbyter only in the mouth of Perpetua. This is probably in keeping with his view of Saturus as priest. However, in the vision it is Saturus with Perpetua who ask the questions to the bishop and the presbyter. Thus, the use of the 1st person plural "we": "And we [that is, Saturus, who is said to

have written the vision, and Perpetua who was "at my side"] said to them: 'Are you not our bishop, and are you not our presbyter? How can you fall at our feet?'" (Musurillo 119-123, ch. 11.4 and 13.3.)

22. See Matthew 19:30; Luke 13:29-30; Rev. 3:21.

23. This point is noted briefly in Frend 364.

24. I have used the translation given by Hummel but I have substituted the word "clearly" for the word "evidently" which best translates the Latin word *plane* in this quotation. *Plane quia nunc vobis in precibus efficacior sermo est et ad impetrandum quod in pressuris petitur facilior oratio est, petite inpensius et rogate ut confessionem omnium nostrum dignatio divina consummet, ut de istis tenebris et laqueis mundi nos quoque vobiscum integros et gloriosos Deus liberet.* See *The Concept of Martyrdom According to St. Cyprian of Carthage* (Washington D.C.: Catholic U of America P, 1946)157. See also *Epistle* 76, 7 (*Corpus Scriptorum Ecclesiasticorum Latinorum* [*CSEL*], Vienna).

25. Frend 363.

26. Hummel 158.

27. Hummel 168. (Translator's italics.)

28. See Hummel 169.

29. Hummel 170 (*Epistle* 15, 1 [*CSEL* 3.2 513, 7-13 Hartel]. Translator's italics. See also *Epistle* 27, 3, and pp. 167-171, in Hummel.

30. Hummel 169 (*Epistle* 33, 1 [*CSEL* 3.2 566, 2-12 Hartel]).

31. See, for example, Clarissa W. Atkinson, *The Oldest Vocation: Christian Motherhood in the Middle Ages* (London: Cornell UP, 1991) 18-19 and Schhssler Fiorenza, *In Memory of Her* (New York: Crossroad, 1983) 251-270.

32. Atkinson 19.

# Chapter 5

# An Exegesis and Biblical Intertextuality of the Vision of Saturus

## Introduction

Saturus' description of his experience in heaven contains interesting, if not peculiar, details about the places and the events that ensued. This becomes especially apparent in scene one, Saturus and Perpetua's ascension. In that one scene alone, we are told that: *four* angels carried the martyrs toward the *east;* these angels "*did not touch* [the martyrs] with their hands;" and, that they moved along "*not on our backs facing upwards* but *as though climbing a gentle hill.*"[1] At first reading, these italicized details might appear to be peripheral embellishments--incidental to the overall significance of the vision. However, it is the obtrusive nature of these details, some of which will later repeat themselves within the vision, that catch the inquisitor's eye. Why these specific details? Do they contribute anything to the vision's overall meaning? If so, how and what?

The early church reader would have understood the symbols and read into them their intended meaning. The modern reader, however, is left to decipher their meaning and importance. For her, the text, in this case Saturus' vision, becomes a "network of traces."[2] In this chapter, I follow those traces to the scriptures where these symbols and signs are especially pronounced and the contexts comparable. A study of the intertextual relationship between the vision of Saturus and, in particular, the Epistle to the Hebrews and Revelation will provide the codes necessary to unlocking its meanings. This analysis will show that the intertexts uniting the vision to these scriptures are the interrelated themes of temple, sacrifice and atonement.[3] Other texts, such as the early church writings will also be referenced as deemed necessary.

A textual topographical reconstruction of the spaces mentioned in the vision, in conjunction with the movements performed[4] at these spaces, viewed intertextually, reveal that what is taking place is a heavenly liturgical ritual.

Further, that this ritual is being performed within what seems to be the contours of a heavenly Temple. Specifically, I intend to show that these brief but succinct details, or clues, which include not only places and events but specific movements, numbers, emotions and sense perceptions, point to a heavenly re-enactment, albeit a Christianized version, of the Hebrew ritual of atonement practiced by the Israelites in the ancient Tabernacle and later the Temple--a description of which is contained in the Hebrew Scriptures.[5] I will further show that this liturgical drama really begins in the arena with the martyrs' second baptism in blood and is completed in the heavenly sanctuary at the throne of the God-Christ. Finally, I will show how the vision creates a 'double subversion effect' defying Jewish atonement theology, as well as the Roman state. It is only when these clues are seriously considered that the depth of their subversion is fully understood. A rereading of Saturus' vision shows evidence that there are several layers of meaning that can be referenced, specifically, a literal, or primary and a symbolical, or secondary layer. For instance, in the vision there were "in fact" four angels who carried the martyrs without touching them with their hands toward the east and up a hill. This is its literal meaning because it adheres to the fact or primary meaning of the narrative. But, the four angels are also being used symbolically to signify yet another truth referenced through its second layer.

Because some of the symbols recur in other scenes of the vision, it will be methodologically advantageous to consider the vision's primary meaning(s) first. Thus, Part I will consider the vision's primary meaning. It will focus primarily on scenes I-III. Scenes IV - VI are considered in Part II, which deals with the clues or the second layer of meaning. Through both, I intend to show that the places and performances within Saturus' vision function together to compose a Christianized physical and ritual analogue reminiscent of the Hebrew Temple and the ritual of sacrifice. How these are subversive is considered in part III.

Before studying the vision, let us reconsider it in its entirety. For matter of convenience, I have divided the narrative into scenes[6] reflecting its progressive movement from location to location. Each scene ends with a statement indicating the purpose or effect of the event that took place, and/or is about to take place, at the present or ensuing location. This pattern--the division of the narrative into location and statement or commentary--flows from the text itself and therefore seemed most natural.

**Scene I:** *Airborne Towards the East*

(Ch.11.1-4). But the blessed Saturus has also made known his own vision and he has written it out with his own hand. We had died, he said, and had put off the flesh, and we began to be carried towards the east by four angels who did not touch us with their hands. But we moved along not on our backs facing upwards but as though we were climbing up a gentle hill. And when we were free of the world, we first saw an intense light. And I said to Perpetua (for she was at my side): "This is what the Lord promised us. We have received his promise.'

**Scene II:** *Reception at the Garden*

(Ch.11.4-7a). While we were being carried by these four angels, a great open space appeared, which seemed to be a garden, with rose bushes and all manner of flowers. The trees were as tall as cypresses, and their leaves were constantly falling. In the garden there were four other angels more splendid than the others. When they saw us they paid us homage and said to the other angels in admiration: 'Behold[7], they are here! They are here!'

**Scene III:** *On the Road to Greet the Lord*

(Ch.11.7b-10). Then the four angels that were carrying us grew fearful and set us down. Then we walked across to an open area by way of a broad road, and there we met Jucundus, Saturninus, and Artaxius, who were burnt alive in the same persecution, together with Quintus who had actually died as a martyr in prison. We asked them where they had been. And the other angels said to us: 'First come and enter and greet the Lord.'

**Scene IV:** *At the Temple and Before the Throne*

(Ch.12.). Then we came to a place whose walls seemed to be constructed of light. And in front of the gate stood four angels, who entered in and clothed us with white robes.[8] We also entered and we heard the sound of voices in unison chanting endlessly: *'Holy, holy, holy!'* In the same place we seemed to see an aged man with white hair and a youthful face, though we did not see his feet. On his right and left were four elders, and behind them stood other aged men. Surprised, we entered and stood before a throne: four angels lifted us up and we kissed the aged man and he touched our faces with his hand. And the elders said to us: 'Let us rise.' And we rose and gave the kiss of peace. Then the elders said to us: 'Go and play.'

To Perpetua I said: 'Your wish is granted.'

She said to me: 'Thanks be to God that I am happier here now than I was in the flesh.'

**Scene V:** *An Encounter with The Bishop and The Presbyter*

(Ch. 13.1-7). Then we went out and before the gates we saw the bishop Optatus on the right and Aspasius the presbyter and teacher on the left, each of them far apart and in sorrow. They threw themselves at our feet and said: 'Make peace between us. For you have gone away and left us thus.'

And we said to them: 'Are you not our bishop, and are you not our presbyter? How can you fall at our feet?'

We were very moved and embraced them. Perpetua then began to speak with them in Greek, and we drew them apart into the garden under a rose arbour.

While we were talking with them, the angels said to them: 'Allow them to rest, Settle whatever quarrels you have among yourselves.' And they were put to confusion.

Then they said to Optatus: 'You must scold your flock. They approach you as though they had come from the games, quarrelling about the different teams.'

**Scene VI:** *Conclusion*

46  The Subversive Role of Visions in Early Christian Martyrs

(Ch.13.7-8). And it seemed as though they wanted to close the gates. And there we began to recognize many of our brethren, martyrs among them. All of us were sustained by a most delicious odour that seemed to satisfy us. And then I woke up happy.

## PART I: The First Layer, Or Primary Meanings Considered

### SCENE I, Airborne Towards the East

(Chap. 11:1-4). But the blessed Saturus also made known his own vision and he has written it out with his own hand. We had died, he said, and had put off the flesh, and we began to be carried towards the east by four angels who did not touch us with their hands. But we moved along not on our backs facing upwards but as though we were climbing up a gentle hill. And when we were free of the world, we first saw an intense light. And I said to Perpetua (for she was at my side): "This is what the Lord promised us. We have received his promise.'

The only spoken words in this scene is Saturus' statement to Perpetua. This pithy statement, along with the events that set the stage, however, summarize what is taking place--the experience of the fulfillment of a promise made to them (as followers of Christ) by their Lord.[9] According to the vision, Saturus and Perpetua have not died but have simply "put off the flesh" and have received that about which they had heard but knew only through faith. When we recall that Saturus was Perpetua's (and the other catechumens') teacher,[10] then the demonstrative "this" (*hoc*) that begins his statement takes on a pedagogical dimension and the statement becomes an exclamation. "*This*," her teacher Saturus seems to exclaim, "is that 'promise' about which I tried to teach you but found so difficult because words were so inadequate."[11] The teacher Saturus is now able, (at least within the vision) through the use of divine visual and sensorial aids, to show Perpetua what must have seemed impossible to describe with human words. No further explanations are now necessary. Saturus' task as catechist has now ended.

The meaning of the reference to "the Lord's promise" is assumed to be understood by the Christian hearer/reader, for whom it was intended. In fact, in the Epistle to the Hebrews (10:32-39) we find almost an exact parallel to these words. Moreover, the context in Hebrews is one of struggles, sufferings, abuse, persecution and imprisonment--situations all too familiar to the Christians of Carthage. After admonishing the Hebrews not to abandon their confidence which "brings a great reward," the writer states: "For you need endurance, so that when you have done the will of God, you may receive what was promised....But we are not of those who draw back to perdition, but of those who have faith to the preservation of the soul."[12] According to Hebrews, "what was promised" is the preservation of the soul. What this entails is further defined in Hebrews 11 as the opportunity to "be made perfect" and "live in a city" prepared by God.[13]

The promise of perfection lived out in the city prepared by God is eschatological. In Saturus' vision, the "taking off of the flesh" (i.e. the preservation of the soul) and being carried towards the east and to the place of light (the heavenly abode) is in accord with the definition and eschatological dimension of this text. Saturus and Perpetua have been saved, that is, they have passed from death to new life, from mortality to immortality, from their finite earthly existence to their new and eternal home. Furthermore, through their deaths the martyrs have fulfilled the precondition of "faith" that Hebrews implies is only displayed by doing God's will. In the visions of the martyrs, their triumphant witness that ends in their deaths is confirmed as the will of God who, in the words of one of the martyrs, "will be inside me [and] suffer for me, just as I shall be suffering for him."[14] Thus, "what was promised" can be defined as an eschatological salvation that is directly related to Saturus and Perpetua's pending act of faith through martyrdom.

The *experience* of the promise, however, remains in the realm of faith for all other Christians still awaiting their own journey. Nonetheless, given the authority of visions among Christians,[15] the vision functions as a divine epiphany affirming the fulfillment of the hope that, according to the vision, belongs to the faithful.

## SCENE II, Reception at the Garden

> (Ch.11.4-7a). While we were being carried by these four angels, a great open space appeared, which seemed to be a garden, with rose bushes and all manner of flowers. The trees were as tall as cypresses, and their leaves were constantly falling. In the garden there were four other angels more splendid than the others. When they saw us they paid us homage and said to the other angels in admiration: 'Behold, they are here! They are here!'

In this scene we begin to have a sensorial glimpse of what seems to be the martyrs' entrance into a heavenly garden. All seems to be in expectation of their arrival--rose bushes and all manner of flowers are in bloom, probably filling the garden with a rainbow of colors and sweet perfume. Even the tall cypresses seem to hail their coming by showering them with an endless, and probably colorful, cascade of leaves.[16] But heaven's angels also prepare for and anxiously await the martyrs' arrival. Four angels, "more splendid" than the other first ones, join nature's majestic welcome of colors and aromas with their exclamation: "Behold, they are here! They are here!"

Like scene I, scene II is mostly descriptive. And, in the form of the narrative style of scene I, it also ends with an exclamation. However, there is a change of speaker. This time the speakers are the angels who greet Saturus and Perpetua and act as their hosts. Their double exclamation, "Behold, they are here! They are here!," has several important functions. The first is suggested by Cecil Robeck who believes it functions as a divine oracle. The other stems from the exclamation's emphasis on space and location (i.e. Behold, they are *here. Ecce sunt, ecce sunt)*, and its indirect reference to the anticipation and fulfillment of an event in time. We begin by discussing its function as an oracle.

In his book, *Prophecy in Carthage,* Robeck argues that the angels' exclamatory words may function as a prophetic oracle reiterating "a word of comfort or assurance--to Perpetua at least--that she and Saturus have been and, therefore, will be (in the sense of a kind of historic future) successful in their martyrdom."[17] However, "whether these words constitute any prophetic oracle as such or they constitute nothing more than a simple observation," he states, "is not immediately clear."[18]

That the angels' words function as a prophecy foretelling their successful martyrdom is likely. As stated previously, visions were considered divine revelations of the hidden or yet unknown. Thus, the angels' statement, coupled with the vision of their entrance into heaven after "putting off of the flesh," could very well have functioned as a divine revelation foretelling their victory.

However, I believe the angels' double exclamation "Behold, they are here! They are here!" does more. It also functions as an indication of location and space, the importance of which is better perceived when we consider Saturus and Perpetua's' situation of estrangement from the earthly place they once knew to be home.[19] The connection between personhood and land is ancient. The Hebrew Scriptures, for example, connect nationhood with the promise of land (i.e. Canaan).[20] The exodus of the Israelites from Egypt leads them through the Red Sea, the desert and, finally, to the promised land where they establish themselves as a people. Centuries later, when the Israelite exiles in Babylon were asked by their captors to sing the songs of Zion, one of them responds by way of a poetic lamentation and clamor for his homeland:

> How could we sing the Lord's songs in a foreign land? If I forget you, O Jerusalem, let my right hand wither! Let my tongue cling to the roof of my mouth, if I do not remember you, if I do not set Jerusalem above my highest joy.[21]

The curses he calls upon himself, should he forget his homeland, are included in the Hebrew scriptures as being representative of the feelings of the exiled Israelites with whom he wept "by the rivers of Babylon."[22]

In the Christian Scriptures, (especially in reference to ministry to the Gentiles) the idea of land and identity is disjoined. Christians are said to be in this world "but not of this world."[23] In contrast to the Hebrew Scriptures, the Christian's identity is no longer tied to her or his homeland, but to the Christ whom she or he claims as Savior and Lord. To be a Christian is to exchange citizenship in this world for citizenship in heaven.[24] In the anonymous letter of the church of Rome to the church of Corinth, commonly called *Clement's First Letter*, for instance, the author refers to his church as "the church of God, living *in exile* in Rome" and his intended audience as "the church of God, *exiled* in Corinth."[25] The *Shepherd of Hermas*,[26] considered scripture by most early Christians, reminded believers that they were "strangers in a strange land:"

> 'Do you not know,' the shepherd said, 'being servants of God, you are as strangers in a strange land? Your city is far from this city. Why then, you who yearn for the far city, do you keep vain dwellings here? How can those who hold earthly possessions ever journey to the true city?...Take heed that it may not be profitable to deny your law [i.e. "the law of your true city"] for if you yearn to return to the true city your denial may bar you. So prepare no more than what is sufficient, and be ready to depart contentedly if the ruling lord orders you away. Take heed that you serve in the laws of God, so cleave your heart to Him.[27]

As followers of Christ, daughters and sons of God, Christians are called to be "strangers and foreigners on the earth," but heirs of "the city that has foundations, whose architect and builder is God."[28]

Finally, the emphasis on the arrival at Saturus and Perpetua's new location also carries with it the notion of a prior time that was anxiously anticipated. And, according to the exclamation by Saturus in scene I (i.e. "This is what the Lord promised us. We have received his promise.") and by the angels in this scene (i.e. "Behold, they are here! They are here!"), the exuberance over the end of a period of waiting and anticipating is mutual--on both the part of the martyrs who finally receive "what is promised" and the angels whose excitement reveals their desire for that moment when they would get to welcome the martyrs home.

In conclusion, the angels' statement "Behold, they are here! They are here!" functioned not only as a prophetic oracle. The exclamation's double locative emphasis, and the theological notion of a new identity or "new being" in Christ--whose home is not of this world--shed light on the statement's other function as an indicator of location. To be "here" (i.e. in the heavenly realm or Paradise, also known as "the promised land" or new Canaan), is to be (in the sense of Robeck's' historic future) finally, at home, where the martyrs belong. "Here," Saturus and Perpetua, as followers and imitators of Christ, are not only wanted but anxiously anticipated. To be "here," is not to be 'there,' exiled on earth, in the Roman empire, where these Carthaginian Christians were no longer welcome. And, as we shall see in scene III, "here" even the Lord--the God-King--awaits their greeting.

## SCENE III, On the Road to See the Lord

(Ch.11.7b-10). Then the four angels that were carrying us grew fearful and set us down. Then we walked across to an open area by way of a broad road, and there we met Jucundus, Saturninus, and Artaxius, who were burnt alive in the same persecution, together with Quintus who had actually died as a martyr in prison. We asked them where they had been. And the other angels said to us: 'First come and enter and greet the Lord.'

Expectation builds upon expectation in this scene. Fellow martyrs who had suffered with them appear, giving Saturus and Perpetua's new home a sense of familiarity and quaintness. For Saturus, Perpetua, and other Christians who may have known the martyrs they encountered in heaven, the vision would have served, once again, as an oracle vividly portraying the heavenly whereabouts of their departed brethren.[29]

Upon seeing the martyrs, Saturus and Perpetua asked them where they had been. The other angels respond, however, saying "'First come and enter and greet the Lord'." This constitutes the end of Scene III.

Saturus and Perpetua's question to the martyrs regarding their whereabouts make us wonder if what they wanted to know was whether their brethren, Jucundus, Saturninus, Artaxius and Quintus had met the Lord. A positive response would probably have meant that they could look forward to the same experience. In the Letter of Ignatius to the Romans, he expresses every martyr's goal and expectation with ardent passion and unwavering vehemence:

May nothing seen or unseen begrudge me making my way to Jesus Christ. Come fire, cross, battling with wild beasts, wrenching of bones, mangling of limbs, crushing of my whole body, cruel tortures of the devil--only *let me get to Jesus Christ*! "I would rather die" and get to Jesus Christ, than reign over the ends of the earth. *That is whom I am looking for--the One who died for us. That is whom I want--the One who rose for us.*[30]

Saturus and Perpetua's question is met with the response they were likely anticipating--an audience with "the Lord." From the prison to the amphitheater to an encounter with their Lord; such was the martyr's enduring hope and, as the vision attests, their eternal reward.

## PART II: The clues--The Second Layer

### The Garden

The references to the "east" and to the "garden" can easily be connected to the Genesis account of the garden of Eden. Studies done by Petraglio, Robinson, and others have shown the parallelisms and similarities between Saturus' description of the garden and descriptions found in, for example, *1 Enoch*, the *Apocalypse of Peter*, and *Revelation*.[31] In several passages of the Hebrew Scriptures we find that Eden is referred to as the "garden of the Lord."[32] Further, when the garden of Eden is mentioned it is almost always associated with the eschatological hope of the restoration of Zion (i.e. Israel).[33] In the book of Joel (2:3), for instance, the "Day of the Lord" will also bring about a new Eden. Thus, in Judaism, the Garden of Eden came to be synonymous with the image of Paradise.[34] In post-exilic times, the hope of the advent of this new Eden was transferred to a future time or used to represent the "Age to Come."[35] The reference to the "gentle hill" could then be explained as their ascension into the heavens wherein one would find this new (eschatological) Eden. Nonetheless, we are still faced with the question of whether this idea of a "new Eden" was also part of Christian Carthaginian theology and what may have been the source of influence.

As mentioned above, Jewish visions which include clear references to Eden, especially in its eschatological form of 'Paradise,' are found in *1 Enoch*, a work known as one of the more important Jewish pseudepigrapha.[36] In Enoch's vision, the seer is said to have crossed "far towards the east." "And I came to the Garden of Righteousness, and saw beyond those trees many large trees growing there and of goodly fragrance, large, very beautiful and glorious...."[37] The reader will note that, in accordance to its eschatological use, it is referred to there as the "Garden of Righteousness." But, *1 Enoch* is also important for its influence within the Christian Scriptures and the emerging Christian church. A portion of *Enoch*, for instance, is quoted in the Epistle of Jude.[38] The *Epistle of Barnabas*, written between 70 and 100 of our era, quotes yet another passage from *1 Enoch* as 'Scripture.'[39] Tertullian, himself a Carthaginian, along with other Christians of his time also regarded *1 Enoch* as Scripture.[40]

Tertullian's regard for *1 Enoch* as scripture is telling. This work's popularity among important Carthaginian church leaders such as Tertullian and its explicit mention in the Epistle of Jude (a letter, thought by Eusebius and others of the early church to be addressed to Christian Jews or Jews of the Diaspora)[41] leads us to assume that it would have been read by the teacher Saturus (or by the writer/compiler of the vision) whom, it has been well argued, may have been a "contemporary, friend or disciple of Tertullian."[42] In addition, one can assume that, as a catechist, Saturus would have been familiar with such an important and popular work.

The garden of Eden as that future Paradise seen in Saturus' vision is not, however, a dominant image within the Christian Scriptures. The primary metaphor for the image of Paradise is not the garden, but the "new Jerusalem," which, according to the vision of the seer of the book of Revelation, is called the "city of my God" by the divine revealer.[43] The paucity of images that refer to the Garden of Eden as the primary metaphor for the images of Paradise within the Christian Scriptures might, on the surface, seem problematic (to my hypothesis regarding the garden). However, the predominance of the theme of the "new Jerusalem" in the Christian Scriptures over that of the new Garden of Eden positively underscores the influence of Jewish eschatological images (i.e. the garden contained in the visions of *I Enoch* and the others) upon the Christians in Carthage and especially upon the vision of Saturus.

**The Missing Tree**

As Petraglio has indicated, there still remains the problem of the absence of any reference to the "tree of life" in the vision of Saturus.[44] He further notes that there is no mention of Saturus and Perpetua going to eat of this tree which he believes that martyrs would have "had a right" to, according to Rev. 2:7 and 22:14.[45] This factor is important because in the visions of Enoch, Peter and the seer of Patmos, the tree and its role and function within the garden is predominant. In the book of Revelation the "garden of God"[46] is always mentioned in conjunction with "the tree of life"[47] whose leaves are "for the healing of the nations."[48] In the visions of Enoch and Peter, the importance of the garden centers around the presence and access to the tree of life (also called tree of wisdom) by the risen faithful:

> And I came to the Garden of Righteousness, and saw beyond those trees many large trees...and the tree of wisdom whereof they eat and know wisdom. That tree is in height like the fir, and its leaves are like (those of) the Carob tree: and its fruit is like the clusters of the vine, very beautiful; and the fragrance of the tree, and how attractive is its look.' Then Raphael, the holy angel who was with me, answered me, and said: 'This is the tree of wisdom, of which thy father old (in years) and thy aged mother, who were before thee, have eaten, and they learnt wisdom and their eyes were opened, and they knew that they were naked and they were driven out of the garden.'[49]

As can be seen, the role of the tree of life within the garden is central to the text. Not only is the tree important for its gift (fruit) of wisdom, the tree also stands as a historical and divine marker eternally pointing to "thy father old (in years) and thy aged mother['s]" disobedience and God's restoring mercy upon the progeny of Adam and Eve. In addition, the tree is also beautiful to behold. This is further illustrated within the text:

> I saw all the sweet-flowering trees....And in the midst of the trees that of life, in that place whereon the Lord rests, when He goes up into paradise; and this tree is of ineffable goodness and fragrance, and adorned more than every existing thing; and on all sides it is in form gold-looking and vermilion and fire-like and covers all, and it has produce from all fruits. Its root is in the garden at the earth's end.[50]

The tree also plays a central role in the *Apocalypse of Peter*. In his vision, Peter is shown the whereabouts of the "righteous fathers":

> And he showed us a large open garden with a pleasant tree in which fruit gave blessing and....and on the tree I saw a miracle happen: new fruit was appearing constantly.[51]

From the emphasis placed on the tree of life within the above texts, one can easily conclude that in the visions ascribed to Peter, Enoch and John of Patmos, the tree is axiomatic to the function and role of the garden. Among its distinctive qualities is its wisdom-giving fruit, its role and function as a historical marker reminding the beholder of God's mercy, and its unique beauty. This leads us to ask why the tree is absent from the vision of Saturus, especially if, as we have shown above, the garden in the vision represents the Garden of Eden.

The question of the absence of the tree of life within the vision might be solved if we consider the vision of the garden to reflect that stage prior to the "end of the age" when the spiritual, natural and political calamities imaginatively portrayed in Revelation (but also in the Hebrew scriptures and throughout the New Testament) will have transpired. Tertullian refers to this stage as the "present age" or the time of "general history" that needs to come to pass before the "the end of the age."[52] This stage is particularly marked by the absence of the great judgment which ushers in the end of time and history as we know it.[53] Following the end of time and history (also known as the apocalypse) the faithful are rewarded with a new creation--the new heaven and the new earth--wherein they are to reign eternally with God (21-22). It is at this stage that the heavenly Jerusalem is finally established in all its plenitude--with the throne of God and the river of the water of life flowing from it through the middle of the street of the city and, with the tree of life standing on either side of that river (22:1-2). Glory, temple and heaven become one.[54] There is no longer need for a temple "for its temple is the Lord God"[55] and, unlike the earthly Jerusalem, "its gates will never be shut by day, and there will be no night there."[56] In this stage, as Aelred Cody points out, there are no rites and formularies--all "liturgical action [and their earthly liturgical counterpart] has given way to the simple but rich presence of the whole Church before God."[57]

Saturus' historical context would have indicated to him that the end times was not yet a historical reality. This is especially evident in scene V where the bishop Optatus and the presbyter Aspasius, whose congregations are in strife, ask for Saturus and Perpetua's mediation: "Make peace between us. For you have gone away and left us thus."[58] Unlike the other martyrs and saints in Saturus' vision "who have gone away" (i.e. to be with God), the bishop and the presbyter are very much alive.[59] This would explain why they said to Saturus and Perpetua that "you have gone away and left us thus," and why the angels would tell Optatus to tend to earthly (ecclesiastical) matters by scolding his flock for "they approach you as though they had come from the games, quarreling about the different teams."[60] The bishop, the presbyter, and their congregation are still an earthly-bound congregation. This would at least indicate that the "healing of the nations," for which the tree of life was intended, was not yet a possibility since the new Jerusalem depicted in Revelation 21 and 22 by the seer of Patmos was still in the eschatological future.

This view is fortified when we consider whether or not Saturus was a *dispensationalist*, a modern term for the ancient belief that God has divided God's dealings with humanity into periods, ages or dispensations. This belief found support in the Hebrew and Christian Scriptures and in various important Christian writers, including Papias,[61] Irenaeus,[62] Justin Martyr,[63] and Tertullian. Tertullian's *De Carnis Resurrectione*, thought to be written between 200 and 206--before his conversion to Montanism, gives a clear picture of the nature of this dispensational belief. In the excerpt that follows, he delineates "the order of history" beginning with Jewish history until the destruction of Jerusalem, followed by general history until the advent of the "Last Day," the day of "wrath and repayment" that ushers forth the end of the age:

> Since, however, *even the seasons for all our hope are fixed* by the holy writings,--at the Advent, I take it, of Christ,--and they may not be fixed earlier, our prayers sigh for *the end of the present age*, for the passing of the universe too, *for "the great day of the Lord," "the day" of wrath and "of repayment," the Last Day*, hidden as it is and "known to none but the Father," and yet indicated beforehand by "signs and portents" and clashes of elements and "collisions of nations...." When asked by His [Jesus'] pupils when those things were to happen which He had meantime blurted out about the end of the temple, He sets forth *the order of history, first Jewish history till the destruction of Jerusalem, then general history till the end of the age*. For after He had proclaimed: "and then will Jerusalem be trampled upon by the heathen, until the history of the heathen be completed," who are of course to be selected by God and to be collected along with the remainder of Israel, then for the world and for the age He preaches, according to Joel and Daniel and the whole council of prophets, the "signs" that will come to pass "in the sun and moon and stars, the end of the heathen, with stupefaction at the roar of the sea, and the movement of men turning cold with terror and waiting for those things that threaten the world. For the powers of the heavens," He says, "shall be shaken, *and then shall they see the Son of Man coming on the clouds with much power and glory.*[64]

Only when these things have begun to take place, Tertullian taught, can the believers "come forth and raise your heads," because their redemption has come near. Should anyone be confused about the times or "seasons," Tertullian reminds them that Jesus said only that the day of redemption was "approaching, *not that it was now present*:"

> And 'when these things have begun to take place,' not when they have taken place, because when they have taken place, then "your redemption" will be at hand, which is said 'to be approaching'....'So also you, when you have seen all

this taking place, must know that the kingdom of God is at hand.' 'Be watchful therefore at all times, that you may be deemed worthy to escape all these things and may stand before the Son of man,' of course by means of resurrection, *all other things having first been gone through.*[65]

Tertullian ends this piece with a series of rhetorical questions (especially aimed at the Valentinians) the answers to which indicate his belief that these "signs and portents" had not yet come to pass. Consequently, "the great day of the Lord, " "the Last Day," still lies within the eschatological future:

> Who, therefore, has aroused the Lord already so unseasonably, so unripely, from God's right hand, "to smash the earth," according to Isaiah, which earth is, I suppose, still unharmed? Who has already "put Christ's enemies under His feet," according to David, being swifter than the Father, while all the assembly of citizens besides are shouting against them: " the Christians to the lion"?....Till now no "tribe had mourned for tribe, " recognizing Him 'Whom they have pierced," no one as yet has "welcomed Elijah," no one as yet has "fled" from antichrist, no one as yet has "wept for Babylon's end"....[66]

Nonetheless, we must ask if the author of the vision (of Saturus) would have held similar beliefs regarding the dispensations. Several factors strongly affirm the probability that the author of the vision of Saturus was influenced by such dispensational beliefs regarding the eschatological kingdom of God. Among these is the popular argument that the author of the Passion was Tertullian or at least a "contemporary, perhaps a friend or disciple" of Tertullian.[67] The similarities in literary style between Saturus' narrative and the editor's supports this thesis. The location of the composition of the Passion of Perpetua and Felicitas is considered by scholars to have been third century Africa[68] thus placing the author within the immediate theological influence of Tertullian and, or Tertullian's ideas. The extent of the influence, especially upon Tertullian's surroundings, is captured by Barnes' statement that "no Christian who was writing in Africa soon after 200 could have escaped the overwhelming influence of his forceful rhetoric."[69] Thus, it seems highly unlikely that Saturus (or the author of the vision) would not have held similar beliefs regarding the eschatological kingdom of God and the dispensations preceding it. This dispensationalist belief might very well explain the absence of the tree of life within his vision of the garden. The absence of the spiritual, natural and political calamities that would signal the end of time and the beginning of eternal bliss in God's heavenly Jerusalem, would have led Saturus to envision a "present age" version of the garden portrayed in Revelation and in the other apocalypses afore mentioned. For Saturus, the presence of the tree of life in the garden would have seemed as "unseasonably" and as "unripely" as the belief that "the great day of the Lord" had come *before* the realization of the dispensations that were prophesied in the Hebrew and Christian Scriptures.[70] A garden without the tree of life whose role and function is destined to be realized only after the end of the age, in the New Jerusalem, would seem most natural. Finally, the appearance of the earthly-bound bishop and the presbyter in Saturus' vision, and the angel's admonition to "tend to your flock" would signal the continuation of time and history, at least for Saturus' immediate future.

## Saturus' Vision and the Book of Revelation

There are yet other clues that indicate that the garden scene is only one facet of the grand liturgical drama unfolding before us. The spaces mentioned in the vision in conjunction with the movements performed at these spaces describe a ritual taking place in what seems to be the contours of a heavenly Temple. Reference to the "east" and the "gentle hill" in the vision are reminiscent of the Hebrew Temple located in the eastern hill of Jerusalem, called Mount Zion.[71] Both the book of Revelation and the Epistle to the Hebrews present a "heavenly model" of Jerusalem and its Temple/Tabernacle.[72] Petraglio's study examines the connection between the Greek version of the vision of Saturus to the Greek text of Revelation.

According to Petraglio, several images in the vision of Saturus can be found within the book of Revelation. Important among these are: the four angels, the light, the white robes, the throne, the singing of the trisagion, and the mention of the elders that stood behind the throne. However, a closer analysis suggests that the analogies seem at best superficial. Petraglio found that the Greek recensions of the *Passio* and the book of Revelation do not use the same Greek terms to describe many of the images that they share in common. More importantly, he discovered that most of the images, especially those within chapters 11 and 13 of Saturus' vision differ in context and function from those in Revelation.

Petraglio concludes that chapters 11 and 13 are in general "very far from the Apocalypse."[73] On the other hand, he found comparable analogies between chapter 12 of Saturus' vision and Revelation chapters 1, 4, 6, 7 with probable influence from chapters 14, 19 and 21 of the same book.

This disparity in consistency between the images in the vision of Saturus and those in Revelation become lucid upon comparison of the "new Jerusalem" described in chapters 21 and 22 of the book of Revelation with the location described by Saturus in his vision. It will help to cite part of chapters 21 and 22 here in order to show the distinction between them:

> *I saw no temple in the city* [the new Jerusalem], *for its temple is the Lord God the Almighty and the Lamb.* And the city has no need of sun or moon to shine on it, for the glory of God is its light, and its lamp is the Lamb....*Its gates will never be shut by day*--and there will be no night there....Then the angel showed me *the river of the water of life, bright as crystal, flowing from the throne of God* and of the Lamb through the middle of the street of the city. *On either side of the river is the tree of life with its twelve kinds of fruit,* producing its fruit each month; and the leaves of the tree are for the healing of the nations.[74]

In the "new heaven and new earth" established after the millennium (i.e. a thousand years of peace under Messianic rule)[75] and the "second death"[76] in the vision of the seer of Patmos, there is no longer any temple in the city.[77] This stands in contrast to the vision of Saturus wherein the contours of a heavenly temple, with its gates and the throne around which the elders and hosts of angels stand singing the trisagion, are made evident (see below).

In the book of Revelation the gates that surround the new city are said never to be "shut by day--and there will be no night there."[78] However, in the vision of Saturus, after the angels admonish bishop Optatus regarding his flock, Saturus expressly adds that "it seemed as though they [the angels] wanted to close the gates." This does not coincide with the new Jerusalem of Revelation (21-22) wherein the gates are to remain open.

Further, we remember that in the new Jerusalem described by the seer of Patmos, there is a "river of the water of life... flowing from the throne of God...through the middle of the street of the city. On either side of the river is the tree of life with its twelve kinds of fruit, producing its fruit each month; and the leaves of the tree are for the healing of the nations."[79] This important image is missing from Saturus' vision. There is no mention of a river of the water of life, with the tree of life on either side, and no mention of its fruit and its salubrious leaves.

Thus, while there are some parallels that link Saturus' vision to the one in Revelation, the (apocalyptical) context in which Revelation unfolds and the important characteristics that make the new Jerusalem what it is--the tree and the water of life--also sets the vision of Saturus and the vision of the seer of Patmos apart. In the following pages, the Epistle to the Hebrews will be referenced as a key intertext. The theological implications of this connection will be discussed in the last section (on subversion).

**The Christianized Analogue of the Hebrew Temple**

From the garden, Perpetua and Saturus walk across "to an open area by way of a broad road" where they meet the other martyrs.[80] On their way to greet the Lord, they come to a place "whose walls seemed to be constructed of light."[81] The entrance to this place is through a gate in front of which stood four angels. At the entrance, the angels don them with white robes and they, along with the martyrs, "entered in."[82] We are told that from this place Saturus and Perpetua could hear the sound of voices chanting in unison "Holy, holy, holy," and they also *"seemed to see* an aged man with white hair and a youthful face"[83] (italics mine). Four angels stood at the aged man's right and left, and behind these stood other aged men.[84] At this point they "entered" the place wherein was the throne upon which they had seemed to see an aged man.[85] Before we begin a reconstruction of the spaces mentioned, we need to refer to the other gates not mentioned here but included in scenes V and VI. They are the gates that surround the garden (13.1 and 13.7) and the gate in front of which stood the four angels who covered Perpetua and Saturus with the white robes.

Thus, beginning from an open space enclosed by several gates, the martyrs walk along a broad street and enter into a room of sorts from which they are able to hear and see, though not clearly, what is contained in the next place. The reference to the "walls that seemed to be constructed of light," "the gate" or door in front of which stood four angels, and the fact that the chanting of the trisagion could not be heard until they had entered, indicate that they were entering an enclosed space. Once past this second entrance (the first entrance was to the garden and the open area with the road that led to the second space), they enter into a third place where they meet face to face with the throne of "the Lord" (11:14) whose description--"an aged man with a youthful face"--would imply the God-Christ.

A closer analysis of the physical spaces in the vision will reveal that what is described here is a Christianized analogue of the Hebrew Temple (portions of which are described in the book of Revelation and the Epistle to the Hebrews). We recall that the Temple itself consisted of three sections.[86] The Israelites entered the Temple through the Porch which opened onto the courtyard.[87] The courtyard led to the other main section, the Holy Place. In the vision, the open area to which Saturus and Perpetua walk by way of a broad road is analogous to the open court which leads to the Holy Place. The fact that they are given white robes to wear may be symbolic of the importance or sanctity of the place they are about to enter. (It is also symbolic of their own purity achieved through the shedding of the blood of Christ.) It is only when Saturus and Perpetua are inside that they are able to perceive and hear what was contained in the next place--the Holy of Holies--the name given to the third section of the Temple. The fact that Saturus and Perpetua could hear and "seemed to see" the God-Christ from this vantage point (i.e. the Holy Place) is significant since, in the Christian scriptures we are told that the veil which separated the Holy Place from the Holy of Holies in the Hebrew Temple was torn in two at Jesus' crucifixion.[88] According to the Epistle to the Hebrews this made the Holy of Holies accessible to all:

> Therefore, my friends, since we have confidence to enter the sanctuary by the blood of Jesus, by the new and living way that he opened for us through the curtain (that is, through his flesh), and since we have a great priest over the house of God, let us approach with a true heart in full assurance of faith, with our hearts sprinkled clean from an evil conscience and our bodies washed with pure water.[89]

The absence of the curtain that divided the two rooms explains why Saturus and Perpetua were able to see into the Holy of Holies.

After they donned the white robes and entered with the four angels into the Holy place, they again "entered" a third area, meaning the Holy of Holies and, this time, "stood before a throne".[90] It was in this room that the Ark of the Covenant stood overshadowed by two carved cherubim with outstretched wings.[91] But, in Saturus' vision, the Ark of the Covenant is replaced by the throne and the aged man with a youthful face, or the God-Christ. This inversion is consistent with the theology of the Christian Scriptures and is especially evident in the Epistle to the Hebrews which explains this change via the Hebrew covenant tradition. The old covenant symbolized by the Ark, is replaced by the new covenant or testament that has been 'sealed' by the blood of Christ--the true and perfect sacrifice.[92] Christ then, becomes the true and perfect High Priest who "entered once and for all" into the real, heavenly sanctuary from where he now ministers on behalf "of those who approach God through him."[93]

After the throne scene, we are told that Saturus and Perpetua "went out...before the gates" where they saw bishop Optatus and the presbyter Aspasius. Reference to the "gates" and to the angels wanting to close the gates[94] alludes to the wall that, according to the scriptures, surrounded the temple. This wall also enclosed the courtyard that surrounded the whole of the Temple proper.[95]

Though somewhat schematic, the visions' references to the walls, the gates, entering the different spaces that lead to the liturgical ritual being performed at the throne, are consistent with the physical spaces that made up the Hebrew Temple--the court yard, the Holy Place and the Holy of Holies. The absence of the various Temple accouterments, especially the Ark of the Covenant, and the presence of the God-Christ on the throne, indicate that this is a Christianized version of the Hebrew Temple--theologically and physically harmonious with that described in the Epistle to the Hebrews and portions of the book of Revelation.

**The "touch"**

In scene I, we are explicitly told that the martyrs "began to be carried towards the east by four angels who did not touch us with their hands."[96] Later, however, in scene IV, we are told that when Saturus and Perpetua were before the Lord, "four angels lifted us up and...he [the Lord] *touched our faces with his hand*. The parallel structure of the two sentences is vividly emphasized by its conspicuous references to either touching, or not touching, the martyrs *with the hands* (there is also a parallel between the *four angels* in the first scene *who carry the martyrs up* but do not touch them, and the *four angels* in the IV scene who *lift them up* to be touched by the Lord). The explicit mention that they were not touched by the angels' hands but, by contrast, later touched by the hand of the Lord would indicate that the seer or editor thought it important. But, why? What does this (i.e. the angels' deliberate act of not touching the martyrs versus the deliberate act of the touching of the faces by the Lord) mean?

The notion of the martyrs' death as an "acceptable sacrifice" to God, in imitation of the passion of Christ, is a predominant theme in the *Acts of the Martyrs*. In the *Martyrdom of Polycarp*, for example, he thanks God for:

> deem[ing] me worthy of this day and hour, to take my part in the number of the martyrs, *in the cup of Christ*, for resurrection to eternal life of soul and body in the immortality of the Holy Spirit; among whom may I be received in thy presence this day as *a rich and acceptable sacrifice*, just as thou has prepared and revealed beforehand and fulfilled....[97]

The theme is also present in the Letter of Ignatius to the Romans where he bids them not to interfere in his martyrdom and:

> Let me be the fodder for wild beasts....I am God's wheat and I am being ground by the teeth of wild beasts to make a pure loaf for Christ....Pray Christ for me that *by these means I may become God's sacrifice*....But if I suffer, I shall be emancipated by Jesus Christ; and united to him, I shall rise to freedom....That is whom I am looking for--the One who died for us. That is whom I want--the One who rose for us....Let me *imitate the Passion of my God.*[98]

According to this, the martyr offers her/himself as a "rich and acceptable sacrifice," that is, as *gift*. The gift of themselves (i.e. the martyrs) is to be presented *first* and *only* to the recipient (i.e. the Lord). This would explain why the angels were not allowed to touch the martyrs, and the angel's instruction to "first enter and greet the Lord."

The idea that the sacrifice must first be presented to God, for whom it was intended, finds an allusion in John 20:17. After suffering and dying on the cross Jesus appears to Mary at the garden. Probably anticipating an embrace, he says to her "*Do not touch Me*, for I have not yet ascended to my Father" (italics mine). This has an interesting correlation with the reference to the angels not touching Saturus and Perpetua before their appearance before the Lord. Could it be that the martyrs, like Jesus, had yet to ascend and present themselves before God?

According to the angels, the martyrs' main purpose and destination after they had "taken off the flesh," is to "enter and greet the Lord." There, before the throne, they are received and initiated into the heavenly realms through the touch of the Lord.

It is only after Saturus and Perpetua present themselves before the God-Christ and receive his touch that they are then touched by others. In scene V, bishop Optatus and his presbyter are said to have thrown themselves at the feet of Saturus and Perpetua. The martyrs are so moved by the bishop and presbyter's action, that they "embraced them."[99] Both the probable touching of Saturus and Perpetua's feet and the exchanged embraces between them happen only *after* they have ascended and received the Lord's touch upon their faces.

Finally, and irrespective of the seer or editor's intentions, the Lord's touch upon the faces of Saturus and Perpetua may have indirectly supported the prevailing belief that martyrs possessed intercessory powers.[100]

The martyrs' intercession before the throne, it was thought, could atone for sins committed by those yet to be delivered from their earthly life. Saturus' visionary experience before the throne may have functioned as a divine attestation of people's belief that the martyrs had a special and direct access to the throne of grace where they could intervene on the sinner's behalf. In this sense, the pure (i.e. the martyrs) were, it would seem, atoning for the impure (i.e. the sinner).

In conclusion, the above scene plays upon--to the point of mocking--human justice, or more specifically, Roman injustice. The cruel drama of humankind's inhumanity to humankind, so graphically portrayed in the Roman arena, is eclipsed by the sublime drama at the Throne and its climax--the Lord's touch. At the heavenly sanctuary before the throne of the God-Christ, those who were thought, by human standards, unworthy of earthly life, and are conveniently disposed of by throwing them to the lions, become the special guests of the Divine One. The religious and socially outcast misfits whose gruesome death once entertained the sadistic masses have gained the heavens and stand worthy to be touched by God's own self. Saturus and Perpetua are ushered in as "rich and acceptable sacrifice" to the Lord who, in turn gives the greater gift--the gift of "eternal life of soul and body in the immortality of the Holy Spirit."

For those that recanted, and many did, there was, either through their own martyrdom or, according to popular theology, through the martyrs' intercession, an open door to the throne.

Finally, we recall that the political and religious intent of the persecution was to force the Christians to deny Christ, bow before the Roman gods (e.g. the Sun god) and before the genius of their emperor to insure the safety and socio-political progress of the empire. In the vision, Saturus and Perpetua do bow, but only before the God-Christ who welcomes them with his touch and makes them part of heaven's household.

The reader will note that in the above quotations the theme of the martyr as sacrifice to God is also accompanied by the theme of the martyr as eucharist. For instance, Polycarp thanks God for allowing him to take part "in the cup of Christ." Ignatius pleads that he be allowed to be "God's wheat...to make a pure loaf for Christ." In the Passion of Perpetua and Felicitas, however, this emphasis is curiously missing. What we have in its place is an emphasis, especially in relation to Saturus' death, on the ritual of baptism, and, in this case, the "second baptism."[101] This emphasis on the second baptism is likely based on several factors: mainly, the development of the significance of the role of baptism; the increasing role of persecution and/or martyrs who were being executed before receiving baptism; the possibility of sinning and losing one's baptism.

The necessity of baptism for salvation is emphasized by Tertullian in his *De Baptismo*. "The prescript is laid down" he says, "without baptism, salvation is attainable by none."[102] In the third century, the period of preparation for baptism was three years.[103] This made the possibility of being "apprehended for the Name," "suffer[ing] violence" and being "put to death before baptism" a possibility. Hence, Hippolytus assures the catechumen that, should this be the case, "he shall be justified having been baptized in his own blood."[104] This is the "second baptism" which "stands in lieu of the fontal bathing when that has not been received."[105] Should the Christian 'lose' their baptism through sin, the second baptism, received only through martyrdom, would restore it.[106]

This reference to the second baptism by the editor, as well as the imagery that supports the metaphor throughout Saturus' ordeal in the arena provide the definitional foundation to understanding the deeper meaning and significance of the throne scene. But, more will be said about this important topic below.

**The Drama of Initiation: The Second Baptism**

**A. "Well washed! Well washed"**

The belief in a second baptism or "second font,"[107] as it was called by Tertullian and others, finds precedent in Jesus' words in Luke 12:50 which distinguish Jesus' pending baptism in blood through martyrdom from his previous baptism in water: "I have a baptism with which to be baptized, and how distressed I am till it is accomplished".[108] The scriptural account of the miracle of the blood and water flowing from Jesus' pierced side was also used by Tertullian as a metaphor for the two kinds of baptism:

> These two baptisms he sent out from the wound in his pierced side [referring to the water and the blood], in order that they who believed in his blood might be bathed with the water; they who had been bathed in water might likewise drink the blood. This is the baptism which both stands in lieu of the fontal bathing when that has not been received, and restores it when lost.[109]

Allusions to the second baptism are found throughout the editor's narrative. We find the first use of the metaphor in relation to Felicitas' entrance into the amphitheater to fight the beasts. (Felicitas had recently given birth to a child in her cell):

> With them also was Felicitas, glad that she had safely given birth so that now she could fight the beasts, going from one blood bath to another, from the midwife to the gladiator, ready to wash after childbirth in a *second baptism*.[110]

The second use of the metaphor portrays Saturus' death by the leopard:

> And immediately as the contest was coming to a close a leopard was let loose, and after one bite Saturus was so drenched with blood that as he came away the mob roared in witness to his *second baptism*: *'Well washed! Well washed!'* For well washed indeed was one who had been bathed in this manner.[111]

The words *Saluum lotum! saluum lotum!* (Well washed! Well washed!) was an expression of greeting used in Roman bath houses.[112] The editor, who has probably placed the popular expression in the mouths of the spectators, plays with this custom using the public itself as a "witness" to the fact of "his second baptism."[113] The mob's morbid commentary, *"Saluum lotum! saluum lotum!"* purposely accentuates the metaphor of baptism--or being washed--by blood.

Finally, we might even say that an interesting allusion is made between the baptism in blood and the dipping of the soldier Puden's ring into Saturus' wound "as a pledge and as a record of his bloodshed:"

> Then he [Saturus] said to the soldier Pudens: 'Good-bye. Remember me, and remember the faith. These things should not disturb you but rather strengthen you.' And with this he asked Pudens for a ring from his finger, and dipping it into his wound he gave it back to him again as a pledge and as a record of his bloodshed.[114]

We recall that according to Tertullian the second baptism was normally to stand in lieu of the first baptism when that had not been received or to restore it when lost. But, this is not the case here. Saturus and Perpetua had received their baptism prior to being martyred--Perpetua while in prison.[115] The occasion of the martyrs' death or "second baptism" was a choice of circumstance--the persecution and their desire to "pledge [their] lives" in order that their "freedom [not to deny Christ] would not be violated."[116] In their role as confessors, the martyrs' preliminary baptism in water was thus superseded by the 'real' baptism in blood in imitation of their Lord's passion. The references likening the martyrs' ordeal and death at the arena to a liturgical rite signifying the second baptism are explicit. But, what is directly referenced within the *Passio* is only symbolically portrayed within the vision. We will now explore how the metaphor of the second baptism, as well as the imagery that supports the metaphor throughout Saturus' ordeal in the arena, is continued in the form of a liturgy at the throne scene. In order to do this, we will need to review briefly the baptismal process practiced in Carthage during the early third century. First, a pedagogical note.

In order to understand the liturgical drama taking place at the throne, we need to do two things. First, we need to understand that both the seer and the editor of the passio understood the vision as a divine revelation--a predictive fact--detailing what would take place after the martyrdom. Hence, although in the narrative the vision comes before the scene at the arena where Saturus and the others are martyred, in the eyes of the seer and editor, the vision scene follows, and is the concrete fulfillment of what began in the arena. This means that the editor and the seer would have placed the vision, or the possession of what it promised, in the historic future, that is, after the martyrdom. This calls for the second step--a mental restructuring of the *passio* on our part. If we place the events portrayed in the vision *after* the *passio,* then the beginning of the liturgical drama begins in the arena and ends (per the vision) at the throne with the kiss of peace.

With this in mind, we proceed--from the unfolding drama at the arena to its fulfillment at the throne.

### B. The Liturgical Drama Continued: From the Arena to the Throne

According to Tertullian, the "sacrament of water" or baptism enabled the catechumen to be cleansed from past sins and enter into a new life through participation in the "mystery of salvation."[117] Symbolically buried in the waters of baptism the catechumen was dead to sin and ascended to new life as a child of God.[118] This ascension into new life required the catechumen undergo a baptismal liturgy that, by the third century, had become highly structured. Just before being baptized, the candidates were required "to renounce the devil and his pomp and his angels."[119] A triple profession of faith and a triple immersion in the name of the Trinity followed. Upon coming out of the water, the nude neophytes (they went naked into the waters) dressed in white robes symbolizing their new life in Christ and their entrance into the kingdom of God.[120] They were anointed with perfume or anointed on the forehead and breast in the sign of the cross with the holy chrism.[121] The *unction*, as it was called, is thought to inaugurate the neophyte into the royal priesthood.[122] The confirmation--the imposition of the hands by the bishop "invoking and inviting the Holy Spirit through benediction"--ensued.[123] Finally, the neophytes were brought to the congregation and allowed the privilege of praying with the other Christians and participating in the 'sacred mysteries.' The kiss of peace was shared among them after the common prayer and before the celebration of the eucharist.[124] In Carthage, the eucharist also included milk and honey, a symbol of the believer's entrance into the promised land:[125]

> Made welcome then [into the assembly] we partake of a compound of milk and honey, and from that day for a whole week we abstain from our daily bath.[126]

Like the renunciation and triple confession that came before the actual baptism in water, Saturus and Perpetua's faith is put to the test more than once in the arena. Their renunciation of Satan and his evil works--in this case, the Roman empire and its intention to make them apostatize--cause them to bear the marks of their confession on their bodies. Saturus and Perpetua endure the scourging of the gladiators, the attack of the beast(s) and, finally, are put to death by the sword.[127] From this second baptism the martyrs emerge triumphant--dead to the world but alive to what was promised to them by their Lord (and previously symbolized by the milk and honey served with the eucharist).

Before their death by the sword, the narrator writes that the confessors "sealed their martyrdom with the ritual kiss of peace."[128] As shown above, in Carthage, the giving of the kiss of peace came at the end of the liturgy of the baptismal rite. That it was included right before their deaths by the sword further affirms that what was taking place was understood by the martyrs and/or the editor, as a liturgical ritual of baptism by blood.

Once in the heavenly realms, the martyrs are escorted from the garden to the heavenly Temple where the liturgy continues. Just before entering the Holy Place, Saturus and Perpetua are given white robes to wear. This is significant because we recall that the white garments were given only after the catechumen had undergone baptism as a symbol of their rebirth or new life in Christ.[129] The awarding of the robes signals the emergence from the baptismal pool--the Roman arena--to the inception of this new life in all its fullness.[130]

Dressed in the white garments, the martyrs enter the Holy of Holies and are "lifted up towards" the Lord whom they greet with a holy kiss.[131] The act of being lifted up toward the Lord carries meaning beyond just the Lord's majestic and holy stature. As the many saints and hosts chant the trisagion, Saturus and Perpetua are "lifted up towards" the Lord becoming themselves part of the liturgical offering of worship and praise.

Saturus and Perpetua's kiss elicits the Lord's touch. The touch of the Lord is reminiscent of the imposition of hands by the bishop upon the catechumen inviting the gifts of the Holy Spirit to descend upon the newly baptized.[132] The touch of God completes the initiation into their new being and into their new home among the other saints and heavenly hosts. [133]

The throne scene ends with the instruction "Let us rise" by the elders and the giving of the kiss of peace. The instruction to rise would indicate that Saturus, Perpetua and the other saints and hosts were kneeling before the throne and, therefore, most likely in an attitude of prayer and praise. This act of prayer falls within the order revealed in Tertullian's *Treatise* stating that after all the candidates were baptized, they were invited to pray with their sisters and brothers for the first time. Following the prayer, Saturus, Perpetua and those present "gave the kiss of peace" and were told by the elders to "go and play."[134] Again, we note that the kiss of peace is given here at the end, culminating the liturgy of initiation into the new life, which Saturus and Perpetua, have now been made full and eternal participants.

For the martyrs and the early church, the visions were not merely oracles. They were the concrete fulfillment and culmination of what began in the arena of the amphitheater. Only when this is understood are Saturus' last words "and then I woke up happy" conceivable. His words provide the perfect ending to the liturgical drama of sacrifice through the baptism in blood. The initiation into the new life that is symbolized through participation in the water baptism (and the eucharist) is made perfect and complete in the 'real' heavenly temple where, according to the vision, Saturus and Perpetua abide until the "Last Day" when the new Jerusalem shall descend and all the nations will be able to eat of the fruit and be healed by the leaves of the Tree of Life.

**The Final Scene: The "delicious odour"**

After leaving the contours of the heavenly Temple, Saturus and Perpetua head toward the gates where they meet with bishop Optatus and his presbyter Aspasius and draw them "into the garden under a rose arbour" (scene V). After the admonition of the angels to the bishop and the presbyter to "allow them [Saturus and Perpetua] to rest"[135] and settle whatever quarrels they had among themselves, the martyrs seem to remain in the garden and within the gates. In the garden (scene VI), they find themselves among other martyrs and non-martyrs, many of whom they begin to recognize. Saturus then comments that they were all "sustained by a most delicious odour that seemed to satisfy us."[136] (His final remark "And then I woke up happy," describes how he felt once he had awakened from his vision.)

It has been suggested that the "delicious odour" may have been given off by the trees or rose bushes within the garden. While this seems the most logical of explanations, this vision's symbolic propensities lead me to argue that its significance lies elsewhere--beyond the reasonable or the logical. Indeed, we find various allusions to a sweet odor or aroma within the scriptures and tradition that fall within the context of sacrifice and offering to God.

First, it is possible that the "delicious odour that seemed to satisfy" alludes to the aromatic "holy smoke" mentioned in connection with sacrifice and offering within the Hebrew Scriptures.[137] According to Old Testament scholars, the use of incense and or frankincense in the sacrifices offered to Yahweh[138] by pre- and post-exilic Israel in the Temple(s) is generally accepted.[139] The emphasis on the sacrifice of the martyrs through the second baptism and the allusion to the heavenly temple wherein all sacrifice is received, makes this reference plausible. In fact, one notes the interesting parallel between the golden altar mentioned in 1 Kings 7:48 (this was part of the vessels of the Temple of Solomon) and the golden altar that stands before the throne of God in the book of Revelation 8:3. In ancient Israel the smoke of the sacrifice offering permeated the Temple and its surroundings much like the delicious odor that satisfied the martyrs. However, the theological context of the vision makes this connection suspect. Saturus and Perpetua's direct access to the throne of the God-Christ reflects new covenant theology of atonement through the self-sacrifice of Christ, the new High Priest. A direct allusion to the sin sacrifice practiced by ancient Israel, contradicts this theological emphasis. Further, it would imply that this sacrifice was still practiced by Jews--a historical anomaly in third century Judaism.

The second option is to equate the "delicious odour" with the "prayers of the saints" which, in the Christian Scriptures, is likened to an offering of incense. In the vision of the seer of Patmos, an angel "was given a great quantity of incense to offer with the prayers of all the saints on the golden altar. And the smoke of the incense, with the prayers of the saints, rose before God from the hand of the angel."[140] Further, in Revelation 5:8 four living creatures and twenty-four elders fall "before the Lamb, each holding a harp and golden bowls full of incense, which are the prayers of the saints." Reference to the plural number of bowls that are full to capacity with the prayers of the saints seems to signify an accumulation of the prayers throughout historical time. It is not inconceivable then, that the "delicious odour" could refer to the "prayers of the saints" mentioned in Revelation.[141] Nonetheless, why the prayers intended for God would satisfy Saturus, Perpetua and the others is puzzling. I am not convinced, therefore, that this is what the "delicious odour" signified. There is yet another option however, that resonates both theologically and contextually with Saturus' statement.

In 2 Corinthians 2:15 the apostle Paul refers to Christians themselves as the aroma of Christ to God:

> But thanks be to God, who in Christ always leads us in triumphal procession, and *through us spreads in every place the fragrance that comes from knowing him.* For *we are the aroma of Christ to God* among those who are being saved and among those who are perishing....For we are...as persons sent from God and standing in his presence (italics mine).

In the Letter to the Ephesians 5:1, 2, Christians are admonished to "be imitators of God, as beloved children, and walk in love, even as Christ also loved us, and gave himself up for us, an *offering and a sacrifice to God for an odor of a sweet smell.*[142] As imitators of Christ's life and death, the Christian too becomes a "fragrant offering and sacrifice to God." For the emerging and early church, in general, one way of imitating Christ was through imitation of his passion, that is, through martyrdom. The Christian reader would have easily understood the "delicious odour" as signifying Saturus and Perpetua's sacrificial death in the arena. In his "Address to the Martyrs" (c.203) Tertullian, for instance, refers to the martyrs as "an odour of sweet savour" and also cites Ephesians 5:2 and 2 Corinthians 2:15 as evidence. He reminds the martyrs that though the prison has its chains, they "have been freed by God." And though "Its breath is evil,... *ye are an odour of sweet savour.*"[143]

Lastly, in the Martyrdom of St. Polycarp, the author likens the smell of the fumes emitted from Polycarp's burning body to a "delightful fragrance as though it were smoking incense or some other costly perfume."[144]

Both the Christian Scriptures and tradition support the conclusion that the "delicious odour" refers to the presence of the saints who, together, become an offering of incense (with Christ) to God and to each other. The "fragrance that comes from knowing him [i.e. Christ]" has spread "in every place,"[145] and especially the heavenly courts where the God-Christ abides with the faithful. Like the heavenly sanctuary in Saturus' vision, the metaphor used in the Christian Scriptures and tradition to depict Christ and the Christian's self-sacrifice (through martyrdom and otherwise) has also become concrete. The concreteness of this "delicious aroma" allowed it to permeate the space and thus "satisf[y] all of us."

This interpretation falls within the vision's context of self-sacrifice in imitation of Christ's passion and, it also coincides with the use of the metaphor in the Christian Scriptures and in tradition. The fact that Tertullian uses the metaphor in his "Address to the Martyrs" shows that the metaphor was used in Carthage during the early third century and, given Tertullian's influence, was likely prevalent.

## Conclusion

> But you have come to Mount Zion and to the city of the living God, the heavenly Jerusalem, and to innumerable angels in festal gathering, and to the assembly of the first born who are enrolled in heaven, and to God the judge of all, and to the spirits of the righteous made perfect, and to Jesus, the mediator of a new covenant, and to the sprinkled blood that speaks a better word than the blood of Abel.[146]

The writer of the epistle to the Hebrews used the Hebrew stories found in the their scriptures, especially those pertaining to the sacrificial rite of atonement, as "types" or analogies of truths he states are fully revealed in Christ. For this reason, he speaks of a "new covenant" mediated by Jesus that has made the first one obsolete:

> There is, on the one hand, the abrogation of an earlier commandment because it was weak and ineffectual (for the law made nothing perfect); there is, on the other hand, the introduction of a better hope, through which we approach God.[147]

In the vision of Saturus, this "better hope, through which we approach God" is portrayed through the vision's appropriation and re-interpretation of the Hebrew symbols connected to the sacrifice of atonement. The references to the east, the garden, to climbing a gentle hill, to the gates leading finally to what can only be the Holy of Holies, with the hosts of angels and elders singing the trisagion before the throne, are used and reinterpreted in light of Christian new covenant theology.

This would seem most natural since the seer/editor was himself a Christian. His role as teacher would have further qualified his theological ability to do so. However, it is important to note that it is possible to make theological sense of the vision without referencing the underlying significance of the symbols and events emphasized by the seer. This makes their presence all the more intriguing. It is my contention that the new covenant theology signified by these details worked subversively against Christianity's alternative religious rival, Judaism. The effect of paganism in creating Christian apostates through persecution is documented in early church writings.[148] However, how much of a threat did Judaism pose against Christianity? Specifically, to the Christians of third century Carthage? The answer to this would depend largely on whether or not there was a substantial population of Jews in Carthage.

The argument for the possibility of a strong Jewish presence in Carthage before and during the third century has found archaeological as well as literary attestations. Based on archeological findings in the cemetery at Gamart that date to the second century and a variety of significant scholarly works that have developed on the subject since P. Monceaux's book (1901), Frend argues that there was indeed a relatively large Jewish community in Carthage.[149] In addition, he notes that various references in Tertullian's writings regarding Jewish customs and practices, when corroborated, "indicate accurate knowledge of the local community."[150] But, his writings also point to the animosity that existed between Jews and Christians in Carthage.

The beginning accounts of Jewish-Christian polemic is recorded, for example, in the book of Acts.[151] The continued antagonism is especially evident, for example, in the *Epistle to Barnabas* (70-100) where the author's attack on Judaism goes as far as displacing the Jews (and placing Christians) as heirs of *both* the Old and New Covenants. That animosity is still reflected fifty (to eighty) years later in the account of the Martyrdom of Polycarp.[152] And, Carthage was no different. According to Frend, debates between Jews and Christians were not uncommon in Carthage. Scholars argue, for example, that Tertullian's references to Jews "show close and hostile contact between church and Synagogue."[153] It is also argued that Tertullian's allusion to Jewish antagonism did not only refer to "New Testament times," as some hold, but that he was actually citing "contemporary Jewish polemic."[154] Tertullian's *Adversus Judaeos* (197 CE) is a direct outcome of this. And, in *Adversus Nationes* (197 CE), as Frend points out, Tertullian "singled the Jews out as the most formidable enemies of his new faith, the 'seminarium' for Christian shame, and he described how a renegade Jew had represented the Christians in hateful travesty as donkey-worshippers."[155]

Whether the seer/recorder intended to add to the polemic through allusions to the New Covenant—as depicted by the heavenly temple and the God-Christ—is impossible to ascertain.[156] However, it is not implausible that his clear depictions of the effects of the New Covenant, that is, Saturus and Perpetua's entrance to the throne of God through the mediating role of Jesus, would have supported Christianity's claim, against Judaism, to the "truth."

For instance, the Epistle to the Hebrews (9:3-5) tells us that, according to the "first covenant" only the priests could go into the earthly Holy Place to carry out their ritual duties, and only the high priest could enter the Holy of Holies, but once a year "and not without taking blood that he offers for himself and for the sins committed unintentionally by the people. However, in the vision of Saturus, he and Perpetua are able to enter both the (heavenly) Holy Place and the Holy of Holies. Within the New Covenant, as defined in the Epistle to the Hebrews, the Christian is taught that she or he can enter the sanctuary by the blood of Jesus which opened the way through the curtain.[157] Therefore, the Christian has no need of offering sacrifices according to "the law" of the Hebrew Scriptures. Saturus and Perpetua's confident entrance into the heavenly sanctuary and their visionary witness to the throne of God, the other saints, and heavenly hosts, controverts the Jewish understanding of the ritual of atonement and the Jewish commitment to what Christianity viewed as the *Old* Covenant.

Against Jewish teaching, the presence of the martyrs' at the throne of God reflects the Christian belief that Christ has "set things right" once and for all, thereby eradicating the need for other expiatory/atonement sacrifices.[158] Because Jesus is "mediator of a new covenant," Perpetua and Saturus are able to come "to the sprinkled blood that speaks a better word than the blood of Abel." Thus, in the vision, the underlying New Covenant theology emphasizes the abrogation of the Old, resulting in no less than the presence of *gentiles* at the Throne! Jewish atonement theology is displaced by New Covenant theology and, according to the vision, the earthly polemic finds resolution at the throne where the "unclean" are made fit to commune with the Divine.

The next chapter explores how this communing with God was thought to allow for the bestowing of special favors by God, especially on behalf of the martyr, even to granting the priestly power of the keys (i.e. to "loose and to bind"). This will be explored particularly through Perpetua's visions of her deceased brother Dinocrates and their relationship to her role and function within the rest of the *passio*.

# Notes

1. Musurillo 119, ch.11.2-3.

2. Willem S. Vorster, "Intertextuality and Redaktionsgeschichte," *Intertextuality in Biblical Writings: Essays in Honour of Bas van Iersel*, ed. Sipke Draisma (Kampen:Uitgeversmaatschappij J. H. Kok, 1989) 21.

3. I am using the term *intertext* as described by Vorster, to refer to a specific theme, in this case temple-sacrifice-atonement, which is "the intertext within which other texts of similar content function and point to." "Birth stories, for example, point to other birth stories" (21).

4. I am using the term "performance" rather than "actions," or "activities," for instance, because it helps to illustrate that the actions or movements that take place are specific to the roles prescribed by the liturgical ritual being enacted.

5. See, for instance, I Kings 6: 2-36; 7: 13-51, and its parallel in 2 Chron. 3: 3-5: 1 which differs in some details from its earlier blueprint. Note, the temple described in the book of Ezek. 40: 1-43 is an ideal temple, an imaginary construction, not an actual one. See also, H. H. Rowley, *Worship in Ancient Israel: Its Forms and Meaning* (Philadelphia: Fortress, 1967) and Mehahem Haran, *Temples and Temple-Service in Ancient Israel: An Inquiry into the Character of Cult Phenomena and the Historical Setting of the Priestly School* (Oxford: Clarendon, 1978) 43-48.

6. The translation, except where noted, and the breakdown of the chapters, is taken from Herbert Musurillo, ed., *The Acts of the Christian Martyrs* (Oxford: Clarendon, 1972) 119-121. The titles which introduce each scene however are mine and are given only to help the reader. See Appendix for the Latin.

7. I have used *behold* instead of the word *why* used by Musurillo to translate the Latin *ecce* (i.e. *Ecce sunt*). See 121, Ch 11.8.

8. The Latin A and C texts read *qui introeuntes vestierunt stolas candidas* or, as in Musurillo, "who entered in and put on white robes". The Greek text and the Latin text B, on the other hand, read _νέδυσαν_μ_ς λευκάς στολάς and, *introeuntes et nos vestiti stolas candidas*, respectively. I am following the translation by W. H. Shewring who relies on the Latin text A but also gives consideration to the readings of BCMg. Both Daniélou and Petraglio argue for the martyrs, and not the angels, as the ones who dress in white robes. See Shewring's *The Passion of SS. Perpetua and Felicity MM: A*

*New Edition and Translation of the Latin Text Together with the Sermons of S. Augustine Upon These Saints* (London: Sheed, 1931) xxviii and 33; Jean Daniélou, *The Origins of Latin Christianity: A History of Early Christian Doctrine before the Council of Nicea* (Philadelphia: Westminster, 1977) 3:61; and R. Petraglio, "Des Influences de l'Apocalypse dans la 'Passio Perpetuae' 11-13," *L'Apocalypse de Jean: Traditions Exégétiques et Iconographiques IIIe-XIIIe Siècles*, ed. R. Petraglio et al. (Genève: Droz, 1979) 23.

9. See John 14:3.

10. See ch. 3 of this dissertation on Saturus' status.

11. Robeck: "The promise to which Saturus refers need have no relation to the light at all, but only to the journey upon which he and Perpetua have embarked" (75).

12. _πομονη_ς γ_ρ _χετε χρείαν _να τ_ θέλημα το_ θεο_ποιήσαντες κομίσησθε τ_ν _παγγελιαν.....μεις δ_ ο_κ _σμεν _ποστολ_ς ε_ς _πώλειαν _ λλ_ πίστεως ε_ς περιποίησιν ψυχ_ς.

13. Heb. 11: 16, 39. See also 2 Pet. 3:13 and 2 Pet. 1:4.

14. Musurillo 123-125.

15. See ch. 2 where I discuss the authority of visions and the prophetic role of martyrs.

16. Robinson recommends that the Latin verb *cadebant*, referring to the leaves of the tree (*quarum folia cadebant sine cessatione*), be emended to read *canebant*--The trees in heaven were always singing. Since this does not necessarily pertain to my thesis, I have chosen to follow the translation as is. "The Passion of S. Perpetua," *Texts and Studies: Contributions to Biblical and Patristic Literature*, (Cambridge: UP, 1891) 1: 38.

17. Robeck 74.

18. Robeck 74.

19. Not much is told to us about Saturus' family life, but we know that Perpetua had a new born baby and a family who loved her but could not accept (especially her father) nor understand her decision to relinquish family, friends and home for her faith. See Musurillo 109, ch. 3:1-3, and 113, ch. 5.

20. Gen. 12:1-2, 17:8; Ex. 6:2-8; Lev. 20:24; Deut. 7:13, 11:21, 25:38; Ps. 11:12-13,44.

21. Ps. 137:4-6 (Revised Standard Version). Re: the fall of Jerusalem to the Babylonians (586 BC).

22. Ps. 137:1 (RSV).

23. See for example Jn. 15:19; 17:14, 16.

24. See Phil. 3:20; 1 Pet. 2:11; Heb. 11:9, 10, 13b-17. Note: the notion of "land" or "promised land" was symbolized in the North African eucharistic service through the tasting of the milk and honey. More is said regarding this in this chapter.

25. In Cyril C. Richardson, *Early Christian Fathers* (New York: Macmillan, 1970) 43 (Italics mine).

26. Irenaeus refers to it as "Scripture." In his *Against Heresies* IV.20.2., he quotes book 2, similitude 1 of *The Shepherd*. Also, Eusebius tells us that it was used in public worship. See *Eusebius*, trans and intro. Hugh J. Lawlor and J. E. L. Oulton (New York: Society for Promoting Christian Knowledge, 1927) 66, Bk. III.3.3. *The Shepherd* is included in the fourth century *Codex Sinaiticus*. See Philip Schaff, *History of the Christian Church* 6 vols. (New York: Charles Scribner's Sons, 1887)2: 690.

27. Similitudes 1 and 4. William Jardine, adapt. and intro., *Shepherd of Hermas: The Gentle Apocalypse,* (Redwood City, CA: Proteus, 1992) 75-76.

28. Hebrews 11:10. In his *Address to the Martyrs*, Tertullian refers to this world as a "prison." See T. Herbert Bindley, trans. and intro., *The Epistle of the Gallican Churches* (London: Society for Promoting Christian Knowledge, 1900) 53.

29. Note that those martyred by fire and Quintus "who died as a martyr in prison," in the vision, receive the same reward. See chapter one on who was considered a martyr. Note also that this oracle would have also underscored the martyrs' role as martyr-prophets.

30. In Richardson 105 (italics mine).

31. For parallels in *1 Enoch* and Rev. see Robeck 75-77; Petraglio 19-20; Robinson 38. For parallels in the *Apocalypse of Peter* see Robinson 37-43; Petraglio 85. Also, for the influence of the *Shepherd of Hermas* upon the visions of Perpetua and Saturus see Robinson 26-36.

32. Isa. 51:3; Eze. 28:13; 31:8, 9.

33. Isa. 51:3; Eze. 36:35

34. MacDermot 139. See for example *Enoch* 32:2-3; 60:8; 61:12 in J. T. Milik, ed., *The Books of Enoch: Aramaic Fragments of Qumran Cave 4* (Oxford: Clarendon, 1976) 232.

35. MacDermot 139.

36. For more info. see *The Books of Enoch*; *The Oxford Dictionary* 459. Robeck also points to 1 Enoch as a key source.

37. MacDermot 139.

38. See Ep. of Jude vv. 14-15 where he explicitly quotes and mentions Enoch by name.

39. In the Ep. of Barnabas see ch. 16.4; cf. 4.3 where 1 Enoch 79, 56 is quoted. In Alexander Roberts and James Donaldson, ed., *Ante-Nicene Fathers* (Grand Rapids: Eerdmans, 1989) 1:

40. See Tertullian's *De Cultu Feminarum*, I, iii, 1.

41. See Eusebius' *EC* Bk. III, 38. There was some doubt, however as to its author. For example, Eusebius says that Clement attributed the Epistle to Paul, "but [Clement] says that *it was written for Hebrews* in their own language, and then accurately translated by Luke and published for Greek readers" (italics mine) Bk. VI, 14. The authorship and the intended audience, however, to this day remains uncertain.

42. Barnes, "Pre-Decian *Acta Martyrum*," 522. See also Julio Campos, "El Autor de la 'Passio SS. Perpetua et Felicitatis'," *Helmantica*, 10 (1959):381 where he says: "Si la Passio no es de Tertuliano, arguye pertenecer a un discípulo my aprovechado en ideas y en estilo literario del gran maestro africano."

43. Rev. 3:12. The speaker in the vision is identified as "One like a Son of Man...." who identifies himself as the "The First and the Last and the One who lives. Once I was dead but now I live--forever...." Rev. 1:13, 17b-18.

44. Petraglio 19-20.

45. Petraglio 19-20. Petraglio, who has relies on the Greek recension, points out that the term ξύλον, and not δένδρα--the term used in vision of Saturus to refer to the trees in the garden (11:5)--is always used in the Apocalypse to designate the tree of life (Apoc. 2:7; 22:2, 14, 19). "Evidently," he adds, "one could think that Saturus is alluding to that image of the Apoc. But, this connection is problematic. Indeed, in the Apoc. the formula 'to have a right' to the tree of life (22:14) seems to mean that the martyrs can eat from that tree (as one reads in 2:7). On the contrary, in the *Passio* the martyrs go into the κ_πος where the tree is: but the idea is certainly not that of going into the κ_πος to eat the fruits of that tree" (19, 20, my trans.).

46. Revelation 2:7. "I will see to it that the victor eats from the tree of life which grows in the garden of God."

47. Rev. 2:7.

48. Rev. 22: 2.
49. *The Book of Enoch* (*Enoch 1*), 207(32). Reference quoted in MacDermot 569.
50. *The Book of Secrets of Enoch* (*Enoch II*), 433.A(8). Reference quoted in MacDermot 569.
51. In Dennis D. Buschholz, *Your Eyes Will Be Opened: A Study of the Greek (Ethiopic) Apocalypse of Peter* (Atlanta: Scholars, 1988) 236, 16.1. Note: according to Buschholz, the Apoc. Of Peter was used by Clement who "used it as scriptrue and drew theological conclusions from it. His quotes reflect the form of the text we have in the Ethiopic translation" (29). Although it seems to have fallen out of favor in fourth century (Palestine), it seems to have "retained a more popular appeal" (38). See also Eusebius' *EC* 65, 3.3.2 and 86, 3.25.4-6.
52. In *Tertullian Concerning the Resurrection of the Flesh* Series II (New York: Macmillan, 1922) 52-54, ch. 22. See also Matt. 24: 5-8; Zeph. 1:14-; Isa. 61:2.
53. Rev. 20:7-15; 21:1-5.
54. For an expansion of this theme see Aelred Cody, *Heavenly Sanctuary and Liturgy in the Epistle to the Hebrews* (St. Meinrad, ID: Grail, 1960) 56-64.
55. Rev. 21:22.
56. Rev. 21:25.
57. "Gone are the visions of worshiping (*sic.)*angels and gone is all the liturgical activity of the earlier visions of a heaven when earth was still revolving in history. There is no more temple in heaven, and the sacrifices in the Old Testament type-passage are omitted. The elect are reigning forever in the quiet of the presence of God" (Cody 66 and 70-1).
58. Musurillo 123, ch. 13.5.
59. Referring to this scene, Bueno eloquently states: "Y ahora viene una curiosísima escena que no esperaríamos en estos anticipos de la gloria. *La tierra se traspone al cielo*" (410). (Italics mine.)
60. Musurillo 123, ch. 13.6.
61. Papias is quoted in Irenaeus' *Adversus Haereses,* Book V, XXXIII.4 in *The Ante-Nicene Fathers*, (Grand Rapids: Erdsmans, 1989) 563.
62. *Adversus Haereses.* Irenaeus' own support of dispensational beliefs, especially his millennarian view, comes through in this document.
63. E.g. ch. LXXXI in Justin's *Dialogue with Trypho, A Jew* in *The Ante-Nicene Fathers* 239.
64. In A. Souter, trans., *Tertullian Concerning the Resurrection of the Flesh* Series II (New York: Macmillan, 1922), 52-54, ch. 22. (Italics mine.)
65. Souter 52-54 (italics mine).
66. Souter 54, 55.
67. Barnes 522.
68. According to Barnes, the fact that the work shows traces of Montanist influence but no hostility towards the church makes "Africa of the very early third century...an entirely appropriate milieu for its composition." See "Pre-Decian *Acta Martyrum"* 522.
69. Barnes 522.
70. It occurred to me as I was finalizing this section that the tree of life may also be missing because the author or editor of the vision may not have depended on the book of Revelation for his dispensational belief but on the Hebrew Scriptures (e.g. Dan., Isa., Zeph., et al) and other New Testament sources (e.g. Matt., Luke, I Cor., etc.) where the tree of life is nowhere mentioned. However, the influence of the apocryphal books within which the tree played an important role and function--especially as seen within the book of Revelation--would make the absence of the tree from the writers eschatological theology suspect. Finally, this does not detract from my proposition that

the author or editor of the vision in the *Passio*'s dispensational belief would not have allowed him to place the tree of life in the post-apocalyptic garden prematurely.

71. The importance and sacredness of this site is exalted throughout the Psalms. According to Rowley, "it is not surprising...that when religion was centralized, it was centralized in the Jerusalem Temple" (106). See also Ps 2:6; 9:11; 48.1ff; 50:2; 76:2; 78:68; 87:2; 102:16; 122:3ff; 128:5; 132:13; 134:3.

72. See Revelation 3:12; 7:15; 14:17: 15:5 et al.

73. "Les chapitres 11 et 13 en général sont très loin de l' Apoc. Seuls quelques rares passages de Saturus peuvent être comparés à cet écrit du N.T. Et si l'on étudie de près ces comparaisons, on se rend compte que souvent on ne peut pas voir chez Saturus des influences de l'Apoc." (Petraglio 21-22).

74. Rev. 21:1-4, 22-25; 22:1-2.

75. Rev. 20:1-6.

76. Rev. 20:14.

77. Rev. 21:22.

78. Rev. 21:25.

79. Rev. 22:1, 2.

80. Musurillo 121, ch. 11.8.

81. Musurillo 121, ch. 12.1.

82. Musurillo 121, ch. 12.1.

83. Musurillo 121, ch. 12.2-3. *et uidimus in eodem loco sedentem quasi hominem canum, niueos habentem capillos et uultu iuuenili....*

84. Musurillo 121, ch. 12. 4.

85. Musurillo 121, ch. 12. 5.

86. According to the Hebrew Scriptures, there were three successive temples erected on the same spot in Jerusalem. The temples were those of Solomon, Zerubbabel (called the Second Temple), and Herod. (The temple described in the book of Eze. 40:1-43 is an ideal temple not an actual one.) The spot was the eastern hill in Jerusalem known as Mount Zion. According to Hebrew tradition this site had been chosen by Yahweh. This belief, along with the subsequent sacredness attached to it, rested on the "staying of the plague" performed by Yahweh from that site and "on the presence of the Ark in Jerusalem." "In some of the Psalms it is declared that Yahweh had chosen Zion, and when Jerusalem was identified with the unnamed central sanctuary of the book of Deuteronomy, it would inevitably be thought of as the place which Yahweh had chosen to cause his name to dwell there" (Rowley 77).

The mosque known as Dome of the Rock today marks the sited of the ancient Temple. 2 Chron. identifies Mount Moriah, the site where Abraham was to sacrifice his son Isaac, with the temple mount. Compare 2 Chron. 3:1 and 2 Sam. 24:16 ff. Regarding the plague see 2 Sam. 24: 10-17. Regarding the site from which Yahweh ceased the spread of the plague see verse 16.

87. I Kings 6:3.

88. Matt. 27:51; Luke 23:45; Mark 15:38. Between the Holy Place and the Holy of Holies there was a partition made of cedar wood (1 Kings 6:16) In 2 Chron. 3:14, there is mention of a veil that went before the partition separating the Holy Place from the Holy of Holies.

89. Hebrews 10:19. See also 6:19ff.

90. Musurillo 121, ch. 12.5.

91. See I Kings 6:27 and 8:6. See also Rowley 79, note 6 on the location of the ark.

92. See Hebrews. 2:9, 14, 15, 17; 5:9; 7:27; 9:26; 13:12 and *passim*.

93. Hebrews 7:25.

94. Musurillo 123, ch. 13.7.

95. Rowley 80. See also 1 Kings 6:36. Note the distinct Platonic influence in both Hebrews and the vision, especially its portrayal of the Temple and the heavenly liturgy, etc. For more on this subject see, among others, Cody 77-84.

96. Musurillo 119, ch. 11: 2.

97. Richardson 154 (italics mine).

98. Richardson 104-5 (italics mine).

99. Musurillo 123, ch. 13.3.

100. See prior chapters on this subject. See also, Eusebius, *EC* 144, V.1.45-46, and 148, V.2.5.

101. This is likely because of the manner of death they were made to endure. In the Martyrdoms of Polycarp and Ignatius, both are burned at the stake. The image, therefore, lends itself (in a macabre sort of way) to a metaphor for baking.

102. André Hamman, ed. "Treatise on Baptism," *Baptism: Ancient Liturgies and Patristic Texts* (Staten Island, NY: Alba, 1967) 40, ch. 12.

103. *The Apostolic Tradition of Hippolytus*, ch. XVII, in E. C. Whitaker, *Documents of the Baptismal Liturgy* (London: S. P. C. K., 1970) 3.

104. *The Apostolic Trad.* ch. XIX.2, in Whitaker 4.

105. Tertullian's *De Baptismo*, in Hamman 45.

106. Hamman 45.

107. *Secundum lavarum* or second laver.

108. Tertullian uses this text to explain the doctrinal source for this baptism. See his *De Baptismo* in Hamman 44, ch. 14.

109. *De Baptismo* in Hamman 44-45. See also John 19:34.

110. Musurillo 127, ch. 18.3.

111. Musurillo 129, ch. 21.2, 3.

112. Regarding the greeting see John P. V. D. Balsdon, *Life and Leisure in Ancient Rome* (New York: McGraw, 1969) 30; Victor Saxter, "Les Rites de L'initiation Chrétienne du IIe au VIe Siècle: Esquisse Historique et Signification D'Après Leurs Principaux Témoins," in *Centro Italiano de Studi Sull'Alto Medioevo* (Spoleto, 1988) 7:136; Ruíz Bueno 413.

113. Musurillo 129, ch. 21. 2.

114. Musurillo 129, ch. 21. 5-7.

115. Musurillo 109, ch. 3.5.

116. Musurillo 127, ch. 18.5.

117. *De Baptismo* in Hamman 9-10. See also 30-49, chs. 6, 7 and 12.

118. Hamman 10. Regarding new life or new birth: "Therefore blessed ones, whom the grace of God awaits, when you *ascend from that most sacred font of your new birth*...." Tertullian's *De Baptismo* in Hamman 49, ch. 20.

119. From *De Corona 3*, cited in Ernest Evans, *Tertullian's Homily on Baptism* (London: S. P. C. K., 1964) xxiii. *contestamur nos renuntiare diabolo et pompae et angelis eius.*

120. Regarding their disrobing for baptism, see *The Apostolic Tradition* xxi.3. Regarding the theological meaning of the white robes see Rev. 3:4; 4:5; 19:14. Col. 3:9-12. See also D. G. Dix, *The Shape of the Liturgy* (Westminster, MD: Christian, 1978) 23. See also J. L. González, *The Story of Christianity* (San Francisco: Harper, 1984) 2: 96.

121. Hamman 10. See also Evans xxv-xxvi where he cites Tertullian's *On the Resurrection of the Flesh.*

122. Hamman 7.

123. Hamman 8. Tertullian wavered as to whether it was at the point of the imposition of the hands that the gifts of the Spirit descended on the newly baptized.

124. The Rome, Carthage and Alexandria also included the rite of milk and honey. This was given after the Communion and signified the initiation of the Christian to the Promised Land. Hamman 10. Regarding the prayer see also Tertullian's *De Baptismo* in Hamman 49, ch. 20.

125. Exodus 3:8.

126. From *De Corona 3*, cited in Evans xxiii. *inde suscepti lactis et mellis concordiam praegustamus, exque eo die lavacro quotidiano per totam hebdomadem abstinemus.*

127. Musurillo 125-131, chs. 18.9-21.

128. Musurillo 131, ch. 21.7.

129. While it is possible to assimilate the white robes in the vision to the vestements in Matthew XX, 11-14 (Saxer, 135), the editor's strong references to the second baptism as delineating the (theological) context suggests, rather, the connection between the baptismal robes and the robes given to them in the vision. Also, it is more than likely that by 203, the association between the white robe given to the catechumen who, until then, stood (probably conscientiously) naked before the others, and the white robes given to the martyrs by the angels, would have been easily made.

130. See Col. 3:9-12 and Rev. 3:4.

131. Musurillo 121, ch. 12. 5. See also Rom 16:16; 1 Cor. 16:20; 2 Cor. 13:12; 1 Thess. 5:26; 1 Pet. 5.14.

132. See Tertullian's *De Baptismo*, ch. 8, in Hamman 37. See also p. 10.

133. The symbolism of the touch is explored further later in this chapter.

134. For interpretations on this peculiar instruction by the elders see Jacqueline Amat, intro., critical text, trans., *Passion de Perpétue et de Félicité suivi des Actes* (Paris: Cerf, 1996) 238. See also Petraglio 80.

135. The notion of rest or "entering God's rest" is found in Hebrews 4:1-11. It is portrayed here primarily as an eschatalogical reward--God's promise to the faithful.

136. Musurillo 123, ch. 13. 8.

137. Lev. 16:11-13; 17:6; Num. 18:17, et al. For the use of the term "holy smoke" see Rowley 86.

138. "Hebrews regarded incense as a spiritual symbol of prayer. The Hebrew 'Ketoreth', which is translated incense, means the savoury odour or sweet smoke of a burnt sacrifice. This implies that the object of burning the sacrifice was not so much to consume it by fire as to make a savoury smoke to the deity. Thus an offering made by fire (*isheh*) produces a sweet savour to the Lord (Lev.ii, 2; iii, 16)." See Maurice H. Farbridge, *Studies in Biblical and Semitic Symbolism* (New York: KTAV, 1970) 268.

139. See Rowley 84-86. See especially his note 4 on p. 85 where he includes a long list of scholars who have dealt with this issue.

140. Rev. 8:3, 4.

141. Petraglio also does not support this connection. Instead he states that the perfume is an image that evokes the satisfied condition of the martyrs (21). However, in the argument that follows I show that the Christian Scriptures and tradition, specifically Tertullian's *Ad Martyras* where the metaphor is used regarding the martyrs, gives us specific clues regarding its significance in the vision.

142. (KJV). προσφορ_ν κα_ θυσ_αν τ_ θε_ _σμ_ν ε_ωδίας Or, "...*fragrant offering and sacrifice to God.*"

143. In *The Epistle of The Gallican Churches* 53.

144. Musurillo 15, ch. 15.2.

145. 2 Cor. 2: 14, 15.

146. Hebrews 12:22-24 (RSV).

147. Hebrews 7:18.

148. See, for example, the *Martyrs of Gaul* in *EC* 141, V.1.11 and *The Martyrdom of Polycarp* in Frend 5, ch. 4. The whole controversy over how to treat the lapsed who wanted to return to the church attests to this effect.

149. Frend 187. Among the works cited is Marcel Simon's important study on native African Judaism in ancient North Africa wherein he mentions several Rabbis quoted in the Talmud and designated as "from Carthage." The title of Simon's study is "Le Judaisme Berbère dans l' Afrique Ancienne," in *Recherches d' Histoire judèo-chrétienne* (Paris, 1962), 30-87. First published in 1946 in the *Revue de 'Histoire et de Philosophie Religieuses*,1-31 and 105-145.

150. Frend 192. See also p. 185, note 4 regarding Tertullian's "witness for the persistence of Hebrew among the Jews in Carthage."

151. See 17:5-7; 17:10-15; 22:28 et al. See also Frend 158-159.

152. See Frend 11, ch. 12.

153. Horbury 456. He cites the following scholars: P. Monceux, M. Simon, H. Z. (J. W.) Hirsberg, W. H. C. Frend, and F. L. Cross. See his note 2 on the same page.

154. Horbury 456.

155. *Ad. Nationes*, i.14, as cited in Frend 334. *quod enim aliud genus seminarium est infamiae nostrae.*

156. The vision's references to the hill, the temple, the trisagion, angels, the throne and their context within the vision, would have easily led the Christian (or Jewish) reader to make the connection between these and their Hebrew source and significance. Their place within Jewish life and religio-historical tradition was (and still is with varying degree) paramount. Up until 70 CE, the Jewish temple stood like a bulwark amidst the competing forces of Christianity and paganism as a sign of hope and of Yahweh's promised redemption. Its destruction by Titus did not erase its vital symbolism. The new temple, according to Philo became the soul wherein Yahweh could be found to abide. The Hebrew practice of offering a sacrifice for the atonement of sin, once practiced at the temple and officiated by the High Priest, was not eliminated but transformed. Thus, while the religious spaces and practices were adapted to conform to the new context, the Jewish theology of atonement, in essence, remained the same. For more information see Haran 44-57, 189-254, and Rowley 71-110.

157. Hebrews 11: 19, 20.

158. Hebrews 9:9-10.

Chapter 6

# Mediator, Leader and Advocate: Perpetua's Ministerial Role Considered

Even before her first vision of her deceased brother's suffering condition, Perpetua was confident about her role as intercessor. Upon uttering her brother's name while at prayer, she immediately realizes that she "was worthy" and that she "had an obligation to pray for him." The use of the term *worthy* to describe herself is important. Modern emphasis on God's grace and humanity's unworthiness (e.g. "total depravity") makes her use of the term *worthy* theologically jarring (and probably explains why some scholars have translated the term otherwise.)[1] Why did Perpetua refer to herself as *worthy*? Further exploration into the significance of this term for Perpetua and her community will reveal the source of her confidence. But it will also do more.

Throughout the Acts Perpetua functions in a variety of leadership and ministerial roles. Issues of gender have led some scholars to assume a Montanist coloring. However, an inter-textual analysis of the term and its connection to martyrdom will reveal that this relationship, and not Montanism, provides the basis behind Perpetua's leadership and ministerial functions. It will also explain why Perpetua's leadership role was not only able to flourish, but was welcomed amidst her fellow martyrs.

## Perpetua's Visions of Dinocrates

Some days later when we were all at prayer, suddenly while praying I spoke out and uttered the name Dinocrates. I was surprised; for the name had never entered my mind until that moment. And I was pained when I recalled what had happened to him. At once I realized that I was worthy, and that I ought to ask for

78  *The Subversive Role of Visions in Early Christian Martyrs*

> him.[2] I began to pray for him and to sigh deeply for him before the Lord....Now Dinocrates had been my brother according to the flesh; but he had died horribly of cancer of the face when he was seven years old, and his death was a source of loathing to everyone.[3]

Perpetua's utterance of her brother's name comes to her as a surprise. At least fifteen years had passed since Dinocrates' death, and the mention of his name now brought back the painful memories of her brother's horrible and inopportune demise. She recalls that his passing was "a source of loathing for everyone." The painful images of Dinocrates' gangrenous face[4] probably had caused Perpetua to suppress her memory of him. "His name," she comments, "had never entered my mind until that moment."[5]

Perpetua's statements reveal her belief that she would not have recalled such disturbing memories had they not been divinely inspired. The recollection and utterance of her brother's name was understood by her as a divine prompting; a special call to act as intercessor for Dinocrates. She realizes that she "is worthy," and that she "ought to ask for him." Thus, she begins immediately to pray "and to sigh deeply for him before the Lord."

Perpetua's understanding of her call to intercede for her brother is further affirmed by the context that frames her experience, that is, prayer. Perpetua and her companions "were all at prayer" at the time of her experience. To Perpetua, as well as to the Christian reader, this would likely have indicated, at least, two things: the context of prayer provided the spiritual soil for the work and prompting of the Holy Spirit in Perpetua and also modeled the course of action she perceived was being asked of her, mainly, to intercede through prayer.

That night, Perpetua's understanding of her role as intercessor was confirmed through a vision:

> I saw Dinocrates coming out of a dark place, where there were many others with him, very hot and thirsty, pale and dirty. On his face was the wound he had when he died. Thus it was for him that I made my prayer. There was a great abyss between us: neither could approach the other. Where Dinocrates stood there was a pool full of water; and its rim was higher than the child's height, so that Dinocrates had to stretch himself up to drink. I was sorry that, though the pool had water in it, Dinocrates could not drink because of the height of the rim. Then I woke up, realizing that my brother was suffering.[6]

In the vision, Dinocrates was still a child of seven years, and his face still bore the wound he had when he died. He was among others who emerged from a dark place pale and dirty. All were hot and yearned to drink. At this point, the attention focuses only on Dinocrates. About the others, all we can know is that they apparently shared Dinocrates' dismal (yet hopeful) circumstance.

The number of speculations regarding the identity of the dark hole in Perpetua's vision and the sources that may have influenced it, point to the complexity of the issue. Is the vision describing Sheol? Paradise? Purgatory? Hades? If it is Hades, was Perpetua's view of it influenced by the Hebrew/Christian Hades or the Greek/Roman Hades, or a combination thereof?[7] Augustine, for instance, identified the scene with *purgatory*--that place where Christians were thought to go to offer satisfaction for sins committed after baptism. In purgatory the Christian soul was able to purge itself from its sins before entering Paradise. Augustine believed that Dinocrates was in purgatory because he had defiled his baptism,[8] a conclusion erroneously based on his assumption that Dinocrates had been baptized.[9]

The idea of a place (or *status intermedius*) where Christian souls awaited entrance into the kingdom of God was suggested early on by scriptural passages, and the writings of various ante-Nicene fathers.[10] Their differing views, however, resulted in a vague and often confusing interpretation.[11] It was not until the middle ages that theological speculation regarding purgatory became sufficiently developed and was officially enunciated as Roman Catholic church doctrine.[12] This fact makes any reference to purgatory in the vision of Dinocrates, at best, premature.[13] Modern arguments on the status of the place have provided the reader with other titillating conclusions. Peter Dronke[14] and Franz Dölger,[15] for example, offer convincing evidence that the description of the dark place was directly influenced by ancient pagan literature depicting death and the afterlife.[16] Psychoanalysts, on the other hand, argue that Perpetua's vision of Dinocrate's condition is really a reflection of her own inner struggles and prison experience.[17] However, to conclude that Perpetua's vision of her brother's condition is, for instance, a reflection of her own physical and/or even spiritual and/or psychological circumstances is to read the vision through contemporary (e.g. psychoanalytic) lenses. Because this study is concerned with Perpetua and her community's understanding of the significance of the vision, diverging into a comprehensive analyses of the various arguments would prove unfruitful (I refer the reader to my notes). As we shall see, Dinocrates' status and not the status (i.e. identity) of the place, becomes Perpetua's central concern. It is this concern that is of primary importance.

For Perpetua, the *loco tenebroso* from where Dinocrates emerged dirty and thirsting for a drink, was real. Real too was the pool and its power to quench Dinocrate's thirst and heal his body/soul. Perpetua believed that her brother was suffering and that her prayers were needed on his behalf. This was all that mattered to Perpetua, and the strength of her response to mediate is only overshadowed by her resolve to remain faithful to her call to martyrdom. Not unlike the question of the identity of Dinocrates' location, the matter of the pool's [*piscina*] content has also generated discussions, at least, since Augustine's *De nature et origine animae*.[18] Was it a baptismal font? Or, was it the living water spoken of in John 4:10,14?. Perhaps it is alluding to the unattainable water from which the mythic Tantalus tried desperately to drink?[19] Again, for this study, what is important to note is that Dinocrates' healing seemed to depend upon his drinking from the pool which was, however, not accessible to him. To be so close to the source of healing and yet be unable to access its power was exacerbating both to Dinocrates and to Perpetua. Her brother's incessant and futile attempts to reach the rim of the pool of water and drink grieved [*ego dolebam*] Perpetua who awakened, at this point, from her vision.[20]

Perpetua's interpretation of her vision of Dinocrates is two-fold. Upon awakening, she realized that her brother was suffering. However, she also felt confident that she "could help him in his trouble".[21] Perpetua's confidence is rewarded. Her daily tear-full supplications are answered with another vision.

> On the day we were kept in chains, I had this vision shown to me. I saw the same spot that I had seen before, but there was Dinocrates all clean, well dressed, and refreshed. I saw a scar where the wound had been; and the pool that I had seen before now had its rim lowered to the level of the child's waist. And Dinocrates kept drinking water from it, and there above the rim was a golden bowl full of water. And Dinocrates drew close and began to drink from it, and yet the bowl remained full. And when he had drunk enough of the water, he began to play as children do. Then I awoke, and I realized that he had been delivered from his suffering.[22]

Interestingly, Perpetua's vision begins with Dinocrates at the "same spot" she had seen him previously. As in the first vision, the place takes a secondary role to Dinocrates' condition. Perpetua's previous description of Dinocrates as "pale and dirty" and "hot and thirsty" are now sharply contrasted with her description of Dinocrates as "all clean, well dressed, and refreshed." The ugly wound that once marred his face has been healed. Only a scar marking the effect and the victory over his terrible ordeal remains. The first image of Dinocrates' suffering from heat and thirst becomes completely eclipsed by the overwhelming references to water and drinking. The once unattainable pool of water has now been lowered to Dinocrates' waist and he "kept drinking water from it." One can only imagine Dinocrates fiercely drinking from the pool, with water dripping from his cupped palms and wet face unto his clothes, cooling both his thirst and his outer body. One even wonders if his clean demeanor was not due to his having plunged his small, feeble body into the pool whose water he had so desperately desired.[23] Over and over he drank until he was satisfied.

At this point a new detail appears on the scene. Above the rim of the pool, Perpetua sees a golden bowl also full of water. Dinocrates draws near to the bowl and drinks from it. The indication is that Dinocrates no longer needs to drink from the pool since its function in healing Dinocrates and curing him of his unquenchable thirst have been fulfilled. Rather, he needs only to drink from the golden bowl to satiate his thirst. No amount of drinking will deplete the water in the bowl. The more he drinks, the more it is replenished. At all times, Dinocrates would be able to drink to his young heart's content and always find the golden bowl full.

Dinocrates drank from this cup until he had "enough." Having slaked his thirst, Dinocrates turned to more important things, like play. The implication is that Dinocrates began to play with the water in the pool "as children do." What for Perpetua and the adult reader might have appeared sacrosanct, that is, playing with the holy and power-filled water, is for the child Dinocrates something to explore and enjoy. In (re)discovering the joy and excitement of water-play, Dinocrates [or Perpetua and the reader] also discovers the joy and excitement of his new self.

Upon awakening from her vision, Perpetua realizes that her prayers evoked a change in Dinocrates' condition. The pool was lowered, Dinocrates thirst was quenched and his body healed. Furthermore, he would never suffer from thirst again since he was now privileged to drink from the golden bowl that always remained full. Dinocrates, "had been delivered from his suffering."

## "At once I realized that I was worthy, and that I ought to ask for him": Martyrdom and Mediation

The words, *to be worthy*, are used several times in the Christian scriptures especially to describe the true disciple. In the scriptures, the true disciple distinguishes herself by imitating Christ's self-sacrificing actions. This *imitatio Christi* characterizes the disciple as *worthy* of Christ. In Colosians 1:10, Paul exhorts the church to "lead a life worthy of the Lord, fully pleasing to him, bearing fruit in every good work, and growing in the knowledge of God." Those who do this, according to the Christian scriptures, are considered "worthy" of Christ and are rewarded. In the vision of the seer of Patmos, the Lord admonishes the church of Sardis to:

> Awake, and strengthen what remains and is on the point of death, for I have not found your works perfect in the sight of God....Yet you still have a few names in Sardis, people who have not soiled their garments; and they shall walk with me in white, for they are worthy (_τι _ξιοί ε_σιν).[24]

The few that are found worthy, according to the text, are rewarded by accompanying God in the promised kingdom. In contrast, the person who does not meet the demands of the gospel is called *unworthy* (ο_κ _ξιος). While admonishing his disciples, Jesus warns them that:

> He who loves father or mother more than me is not worthy of me; and she who loves son or daughter more than me is not worthy of me; and he who does not take his cross and follow me is not worthy of me. She who finds her life will lose it, and he who loses his life for my sake will find it....he is a disciple, truly, I say to you, he shall not lose his reward.[25]

The *worthy* disciple reflects her/his depth of love and commitment to Christ through her/his obedience to the demands of the Gospel. She and he prove their love for Christ by sacrificing the love of father and mother and even their children to take up the cross and follow. This text is particularly enlightning since it bears directly upon Perpetua's own situation. Perpetua's decision to follow Christ and to go through with her commitment, even when it would cost her life, distinguished her as a disciple. In deciding for Christ, she severed her dream of nurturing and watching her baby boy take his first steps and grow into a young man. Further, the special bond that existed between Perpetua and her father was crushed by her resolve to choose Christ over her father's love. To him, Perpetua's actions were arrogant and disdainful of all he thought should matter. Thus he clamors with his daughter to:

> Have pity on me your father, if I deserve to be called your father, if I have favoured you above all your brothers, if I have raised you to reach this prime of your life. Do not abandon me to be the reproach of men. Think of your brothers, think of your mother and your aunt, think of your child, who will not be able to

life once you are gone. Give up your pride! You will destroy all of us! None of us will ever be able to speak freely again if anything happens to you.[26]

The father's last words, "none of us will ever be able to speak freely again if anything happens to you," reveal his own inner struggles to understand his daughter's choice. He is so perplexed by her resolution to end her young life and leave behind even her baby boy that he resorts to blaming himself. Only some grave error in his parental upbringing could explain such an unreasonable resolve. As the *paterfamilias* he felt responsible for her and her actions. "Do not abandon me to the reproach of men," he begs Perpetua. If not love, then her gender and her daughter-status should have dictated a positive response to his pleas.

Only his failed responsibility to rear children that were loyal to all things Roman (including offering "the sacrifice for the welfare of the emperors") could effectively explain the governor's order to beat him.[27] The father's persistent cry of supplication, at times kissing Perpetua's hands and throwing himself down before her,[28] must have appeared pathetic and degrading to the symbol of the Roman male and his role as *paterfamilias*. The governor's order to beat him may have reflected his disdain for such a display.[29]

Although the sight of her father being beaten for her decision pained her, she returned to the prison "in high spirits."[30] Perpetua had overcome her strongest temptations--the love for her son, family, and especially her father who,[31] "of all my kin[,] would be unhappy to see me suffer."[32] According to Matthew 10:37-39, Perpetua's decision to lose her life (in this case literally) for Christ's sake taught her that she was *worthy* of Christ, and of being counted among the true disciples.

Belief that this worthiness was specially achieved through martyrdom is expressed early on in the letter on the *Martyrs of Lyons* (177 CE). Concerning the martyr Blandina, the author writes:

> All the wrath of the mob, the prefect, and the soldiers fell with overwhelming force on the deacon Sanctus of Vienne...and on Blandina, through whom Christ proved that the things that men think cheap, ugly, and contemptuous are deemed worthy of glory before God, by reason of her love for him which was not merely vaunted in appearance but demonstrated in achievement.[33]

Blandina's demonstration of her love for God deemed her worthy of God's glory. Thus, she believed that in losing her life, she would find it. So, also Perpetua. Having been found worthy, Perpetua, like Blandina and all the martyrs, "[would] not lose her reward."[34]

Nowhere is this more firmly believed than in the hearts and minds of Christians who saw their loved ones martyred. According to the tradition that developed around martyrdom during the third and fourth centuries, martyrs were worthy of special rewards. Among these, was the privilege of going straight to Paradise.[35] In his letter to the Christians at Thibaris, Cyprian exhorts them to rejoice in persecutions because of the heavenly reward:

and leap for joy, because when persecutions come, then the crowns of faith are given, then the soldiers of God are proved, then the heavens are opened to Martyrs.[36]

Unlike the martyrs, the remaining faithful would have to await the "Last Day" or final judgment when they would be welcomed into Paradise by God, the patriarchs, prophets, apostles and martyrs.[37]

In addition, the martyr had the distinct honor of sitting at God's right side. In the *Shepherd of Hermas*, the woman, otherwise referred to as "the church," appears to Hermas in a vision. "Arise and sit here," she tells him:

> When I heard this I felt dismay that she would not let me sit at the right hand....The right seat is for those who have been found pleasing to God, and have suffered for the Name.....What did they bear?" [Hermas] asked. Stripes, chains, crucifixions, beasts and killing men, for the sake of the Name. Therefore it is given for them to be on the right side of the Holiness, and to everyone who shall suffer for the Name.[38]

Such proximity to God's favor gave the martyrs special access to God's miracles.[39] Thus, it was believed that a martyr's prayer could help to effect God's pardon over the lapsed Christians and reunite them to the church.[40] Even the martyr's ashes were thought to possess healing and forgiving powers. In the *Martyrdom of Fructuoso and Companions*, Christians returned to the amphitheater to collect the ashes of the martyrs "and claimed them for their own"[41]:

> And here too the miracles of our Lord and Saviour were not wanting to increase the faith of believers and to set an example to the young.[42]

Popular belief regarding the martyr's powers would have also influenced Perpetua's positive outlook regarding her brother. She had accepted the costs and challenges of discipleship and believed the gospel's words that this made her worthy of Christ and thus worthy of his rewards. Her role as martyr gave her confidence that she "could help him [Dinocrates] in his trouble" is thus intricately linked to her role as martyr.

But, there is another element that also played a role in strengthening the confidence that led her to believe in Dinocrates' [spiritual] relief. Perpetua had been "greatly privileged"[43] with the gift of visions.

Concerned whether his sister would be freed or condemned to die, Perpetua's brother suggests that she ask for a vision. "You are greatly privileged," he says of Perpetua.[44] Perpetua promised that she would ask for a vision "for I knew that I could speak with the Lord, whose great blessings I had come to experience."[45] In fact, she is so confident that she would get a response that she informs her brother that she would "tell [him] tomorrow."![46] Without further thought to the matter, she continues, "Then I made my requests and this was the vision I had."[47]

The casualness of the latter statement powerfully underscores the truthfulness of her words that she had been in the habit of speaking "with the Lord, whose great blessings she had come to experience." There is no element of surprise or astonishment. The vision was given to her, as she asked, and when she asked.

Unlike her petition for the vision, however, she spends days and nights "with tears and sighs that this favour [Dinocrate's spiritual healing] might be granted me."[48] While she finds herself in a position that allows her to ask for her brother, her prayerful response indicates that what is being asked exceeds anything like a vision. Further, that the magnitude of such a petition could only be helped by her role as martyr. This, coupled with her understanding that her experience of having no control over the utterance of Dinocrates' name was a prompting from God to ask for Dinocrates, worked synergistically to build her confidence.

Perpetua's mediating role between Dinocrates and God's favor is only one instance within the *Martyrdom* where her charismatic gifts and leadership abilities are displayed. As we have already seen, Perpetua's mediating role did not limit itself to Dinocrates. From the beginning of the *Martyrdom*, Perpetua's ability to minister to the other prisoners through her charismatic and leadership skills comes through. The *Martyrdom* is particularly marked by her repeated and noteworthy role as advocate for the rest of the martyrs imprisoned with her. The first instance involves a direct confrontation with the prison officer. According to the compiler, rumors by "certain very foolish people" had made the military tribune become afraid "that they [the martyrs] would be spirited out of the prison by magical spells."[49] Because of this, Perpetua and the other prisoners were being treated with "extraordinary severity."[50] Perpetua's leadership, as well as her ingenuity, comes through in her argument against their unfair treatment:

> Why can you not even allow us to refresh ourselves properly? For we are the most distinguished of the condemned prisoners, seeing that we belong to the emperor; we are to fight on his very birthday. Would it not be to your credit if we were brought forth on the day in a healthier condition?[51]

As a result of her advocacy, the prisoners began to be treated more humanely. Visitors were allowed to visit, "so that the prisoners could dine in their company."[52]

The second display of her strong leadership abilities takes place in the amphitheater before the military tribune. As the prisoners were led up the gates, they were forced to wear the robes of priests of Saturn and the women the dress of the priestesses of Ceres.[53] Perpetua, however, "strenuously resisted this to the end":

> We came to this of our own free will, that our freedom should not be violated. We agreed to pledge our lives provided that we would do no such thing. You agreed with us to do this.[54]

Perpetua stood up to the powers of the Roman state and challenged their injustice. By using the tribune's own legal conditions against them, she undermined the state's subversive attempt to demean the witness of the martyrs. In the end, "even injustice recognized justice" and the robes were allowed to come off as Romans, Jews and Christians[55] alike witnessed what the courage of this one woman had done. Perpetua's words, and certainly her valor, won the martyrs the freedom from being forced to be demeaned by wearing the symbolic pagan robes. Their dignity as Christians witnesses was also restored. Because of Perpetua's role, a greater victory was had, not only for Perpetua and the other martyrs, but for the whole of the Christian church.

The next instance of her leadership and ministerial role happens after she and Felicitas were called back after being attacked by a mad heifer.[56] Still bleeding from her wounds, Perpetua is said to have called for her brother and the other catechumens to admonish them to "stand fast in the faith and love one another, and do not be weakened by what we have gone through."[57] After more pain and torture, Perpetua and the others perished by the sword.

## Martyrdom and the New *Communitas*

In her book, *The Oldest Vocation: Christian Motherhood in the Middle Ages*, Clarissa Atkinson correctly notes that persecution and martyrdom played a key role in the development of a new kind of community among martyrs. This community or *communitas* was reminiscent of the early women and men who followed Jesus.[58] "Martyrdom and persecution," she argues, "undercut the values of the dominant culture, breaking traditional bonds and forging new ones."[59] To support her argument, she turns, among other, to the *Acts of the Martyrs*. These, she argues, "present very different models of family and of gender relations."[60] The martyrdoms of the young mothers Perpetua and Felicitas, for example, "demonstrate the martyrs' renunciation of traditional concerns and reversal of ordinary priorities."[61] Focus on the person's role as martyr, or God's special witness before humanity, also blurred distinctions between gender and status. In this new community of martyrs, earthly and ecclesiastical distinctions between lay and priest, female and male, slave and free were supplanted by their common and crowning mark--their role as martyrs. Catechumen and bishop equally showed their merits by their strength of endurance and commitment to the faith.

Perhaps nowhere are the ecclesiastical and gender lines less significantly evident than in the account of the Martyrs of Lyons. According to the writer, the only distinguishing mark was the Christian's denial or testimony of faith. The bishop Ponthinus of Lyons, the deacon Sanctus, the fifteen year-old Ponticus, Blandina and other Christians are equally praised for their testimony of courage and faith. Neither gender, age nor status ranked above their main calling to be exemplary witnesses to Christ's glory. Blandina's gender was not an issue for the author who displays no theological qualms about likening her crucified body to the figure of Christ on the cross:

> Blandina was hung on a post and exposed as bait for the wild animals that were let loose on her. She seemed to hang there in the form of a cross, and by her fervent prayer she aroused intense enthusiasm in those who were undergoing their ordeal, for in their torment with their physical eyes they saw in the person of their sister him who was crucified for them, that he might convince all who believe in him that all who suffer for Christ's glory will have eternal fellowship in the living God.[62]

The violence Blandina bears for the sake of Christ is lifted up as a sacrificial embodiment of Christ's power over death, his love and eternal reward for those who believe in him.

The analogy of Blandina as a type of Christ is peculiar to her role as martyr. In the future, analogies between women and the divine would be limited to accentuating gender stereotypes such as mothering, nurturing and chastity (e.g. the virgin Mary). The author's depiction of Blandina as a type of Christ powerfully underscores the type of egalitarianism distinctive to the community of martyrs and the eschatological community to which they awaited immediate entry.

Separated from their communities and, usually from their leaders, the martyrs looked to each other for support and encouragement. This encouragement oftentimes came through visions and through the charismatic leadership of other martyrs. The authority and role of the Holy Spirit not only in causing these visions but in selecting the medium or vessel through which to reveal them, was assumed by the martyrs. Charismatic gifts and leadership abilities, not the person's ecclesiastical rank, title or social status, became highly valued by the martyrs who depended and looked to these as immediate signs of God's imminent presence. Thus, these gifts were not only valued but encouraged among each other.

Finally, it is the dynamic presence of this new *communitas* and not Montanism, I believe, that is the defining characteristic. And, within this *communitas* Perpetua's role as leader and mediator would not only have been allowed to flourish, it would have been encouraged.

## Conclusion

Perpetua's leadership and ministerial functions have been thought to reflect Montanist affiliations. Emphasis on the Montanist status of the work has served to demean Perpetua's role, and to cloud other arguments that might better elucidate our understanding of the text. The argument that persecution and martyrdom provided the martyrs with the opportunity, as well as the need, to re-create a community based on egalitarian and charismatic leadership provides a different reading of the text. When one reads it in this light one is better able to appreciate Perpetua's role and how her charismatic gifts of visions and leadership would have been not only recognized, but valued.

Belief in the autonomy of the Holy Spirit to fall on whom it pleased also provided this community with its defining model.[63] The Holy Spirit's impartiality to persons and gender, was exemplified through the spectrum of persons and children who were blessed with visions. The result was a leveling of the hierarchical and gender-based pyramid to include women as well as men.

From the third century until now, the story of Perpetua, Felicitas and the other martyrs has been held up as a shining bulwark, a tribute to the church's saints, strength and mission. Perpetua's story in particular continues to testify to the history of Christian women's advocacy, leadership and ministerial roles, and, to the Holy Spirit's sanctioning of these roles.

# Notes

1. Musurillo, for example, interprets *dignam esse* as "I was privileged" (115, ch. 7.2).
2. Musurillo translates the sentence et *cognoui me statim dignam esse et pro eo petere debere* as, "At once I realized that I was privileged to pray for him." Shewring, however, uses "worthy," which better translates the word *dignam* (29).
3. Musurillo 115, ch. 7.1-5.
4. Amat proposes that what Dinocrates had may have been a leprous ulcer. This, he adds, would "explain the double horror Dinocrates inspired" since leprosy was also considered "unclean" (my translation). For the Greek rendition of the Latin text and Amat's references regarding views on leprosy see 128, ch. 7.5, and 216 respectively.
5. Musurillo 115, ch. 7.11.
6. Musurillo 115, ch. 7.4, 7-9.
7. For a discussion on the possible sources behind Perpetua's vision of the afterlife, see Robeck 47-53.
8. See Augustine's *De natura et origine animae* (*On the Soul and the Resurrection*), eds., C. Urba and J. Zycha, *CSEL* 60 (1913): 312, 3.9.
9. Robinson rightly points out that there is no evidence to support this. First, we recall that Perpetua came from a pagan family. In fact, her father was so angered at Perpetua's confession that she could not be anything other than a Christian that "he moved towards me [Perpetua] as though he would pluck my eyes out" (Musurillo 109, ch. 3.3). Second, we are told that both Perpetua and her other remaining brother had only recently converted to Christianity themselves. In fact, Perpetua, her brother, and the other catechumens received their baptism while in custody (Musurillo 109, 3.5). Thirdly, even if Perpetua had been a Christian at the time of the child's death, it would still have been "improbable that in a pagan household a boy of seven years old should have been baptized." He adds, "S. Augustine's suggestion that the child was old enough to tell lies, and so though baptized to need a period of torture after death, is a mournful illustration of the straits to which a good man may be driven by the exigencies of controversy." Robinson (Nendeln\Liechtenstein: Kraus Reprint, 1967) 29, n. 1. See also Robeck 45-47.
10. For varying pre- and post-Nicene statements (and bibliographies) on the issue of purgatory see, Philip Schaff, *History of the Christian Church* (New York: Scribners', 1887) 2: 599-606; David Blondel, *Traitè de la Crèance des Pères Touchant l' état des Ames Après Cette Vie* (Charenton, 1651); and "Purgatory," *The Oxford Dictionary of the Christian Church*, ed. E. L. Cross (New York: Oxford UP, 1983) 1144-1145.
11. According to Schaff, these "vague and confused" utterances are elucidated by Nicene and post-Nicene statements. For a list of works displaying varying views (2:600, n. 4).
12. "The foundation of the medieval doctrine is found in St. Augustine, who holds that the fate of the individual soul is decided immediately after death, and teaches the absolute certainty of purifying pains in the next life." (see *De Civitatae Dei* xxi. 13) The official teaching on purgatory was ennunciated at the Councils of Lyons (1274) and Florence (1439). See *The Oxford Dictionary* 1145. See also Jacques Le Goff, *The Birth of Purgatory*, trans., Arthur Goldhammer (Chicago: The Clarendon, rev. ed., 1969); Schaff, 600-606; Barnes, *Tertullian: A Historical and Literary Study*, (Oxford: Clarendon, 1985) 78.
13. Barnes regards the idea of identifying the place with purgatory as an "adventitious and anachronistic notion." However, in support of his argument for a Montanist (and therefore unorthodox) coloring, he identifies the place in Perpetua's vision with "hell." This enables him to state that Perpetua's visions of Dinocrates "clearly imply that a martyr (but perhaps not anyone else) can effect the release of a souls from hell and secure its admittance to heaven." How, then, is it that Perpetua sees Dinocrates

in "the same spot that I had seen [him] before, but there was Dinocrates all clean, well dressed, and refreshed"? Musurillo 115, ch. 8.1.

Patricia Cox Miller cites Le Goff's comment on the subject of Dinocrates' location and its possible relation to purgatory: "The importance of the *Passion of Perpetua and Felicitas* in the prehistory of Purgatory should be neither exaggerated nor minimized. It is not Purgatory as such that is being discussed here, and none of the images contained in Perpetua's two visions recur in medieval imagery associated with Purgatory" in "Perpetua and her Diary of Dreams," *Dreams in Late Antiquity: Studies in the Imagination of a Culture* (Princeton: Princeton UP, 1994) 160, n. 58.

14. *Women Writers of the Middle Ages: A Critical Study of Texts from Perpetua (†203) to Marguerite Porete (†1310)* (Cambridge: Cambridge UP, 1984) 1-17.

15. "Antike Parallelen zum leidenen Dinocrates in der Passio Perpetuae," *Antike und Christentum* (Munic: Verlag Aschendorff, 1974) 2: 1-40.

16. Dölger, and Dronke, for example, convincingly argue that the description of Dinocrates' location and his "hot and thirsty" condition reflect ancient pagan cult teachings and lore concerning the dead. Dronke points out that throughout the ancient world it was believed that the dead experienced thirst before attaining a peaceful rest. Thus, it was not uncommon to see libations of wine and water at the tombs. It was also not uncommon for Christians to continue to hold on to such a belief, especially when the Christian scriptures seemed to confirm it (e.g. the story of the rich man and Lazarus). Dronke reminds us that Bishop Ambrose had to desist Augustine's own mother, a devout Christian, from practicing this common pagan ritual. Dronke 11. See also Augustine's Confessions, VI ii, 2.

But perhaps the most convincing evidence for pagan influence in Perpetua's vision is Dronke's reference to the distinct parallel between Dinocrates experiences and those of the mythic Tantalus. Tantalus' thirst, like that of Dinocrates, could only be quenched by the water that was very close yet unattainable. (Dronke also points out that, unlike Tantalus, Dinocrates is not being punished for his crimes and can be helped towards well-being in the otherworld--not by libations but by prayers.") The well educated (*liberaliter instituta*) and only newly converted Perpetua, would likely have read about Tantalus and his afterlife predicament. The similarities between Perpetua's vision of Dinocrates and story of Tantalus are too close to deny Dronke's theory. Dronke 11-12.

17. For instance, in describing the prison, Perpetua writes that she was terrified as she had never been in a dark place" [*tenebras*] and refers to the heat generated by the prison crowd as stifling." Was it really Perpetua that was hot and thirsty" and pale and dirty" and was projecting these feelings unto the vision of her brother?

Marie-Louise von Franz, for example, views Dinocrates, in part, as the personification or the *anima* of Perpetua herself. It is she who has the longing for the baptismal font....Thus, when Perpetua engaged in a conscious quest for the reality of her own baptism, she realized the inner resource of power that enabled her to move with resolve toward her own martyrdom." In Robeck, 53. See also Marie-Louise von Franz, "Die Passio Perpetuae," In *Aion: Untersuchungen zur Symbolgeschichte*, ed. C. G. Jung, 389-496. We recall however, as Robeck also points out, that Perpetua had already been baptized. See also Domenico Devoti, "La Passion de Perpetue: un Noeud Familial," in *Studia Patristica*, ed. Elizabeth A. Livingstone (Leuven: Peeters, 1989) 21:72.

18. For a summary account on Augustine's interpretation of the role of the font in the vision of Perpetua vis-à-vis Vincentius Victor's, whom he opposes, see Kenneth B. Steinhauser, Augustine's Reading of the *Passio sanctarum Perpetuae et Felicitatis*," *Studia Patristica* Vol. XXXIII, ed. by Elizabeth A. Livingstone (Leuven: Peeters, 1997) 244-247. See also Robeck 45-47.

19. As mentioned above.

20. Musurillo 115, ch. 7.8.

21. Musurillo 115, ch. 7.9. 22. Musurillo 117, ch.8.

23. This brings to mind the reference in John 5:4 to the pool of Bethesda. At the stirring of the water by the angel, the first person to step into the pool would receive healing.

24. Rev. 3:2,4.

25. Matt. 10:37-39,42. See also Acts 26:20.

26. Musurillo 113, ch. 5.2-4.

27. Musurillo 115, ch. 6.3,5.

28. Musurillo 113, ch. 5.5.

29. While one might argue that the beating was meant to persuade Perpetua to change her mind, the fact that it happens "when my father persisted in trying to dissuade me [Perpetua]" implies that the father's behavior resulted unbecoming of his gender and a nuisance to his court. Musurillo 113, ch. 6.5.

30. Musurillo 113, ch. 6.6. *tunc nos uniuersos pronuntiat et damnat ad bestias; et hilares descendimus ad carcerem.*

31. See Matt. 10:36.

32. Musurillo 113, ch. 5.6.

33. Musurillo 67, ch. 17. Or, demonstrated in power (τ_ν _ν δυνάμει δεικνυμένην), that is, the power of her testimony or achievement.

34. Matt. 10:39,42.

35. For examples, see Musurillo 13, chs. 11-13; 14.2, and Acts 7:55-60. See also *Epistle* LXXIII.19 in *The Treatises of S. Caecilius Cyprian* 256, and Hummel 122-127.

36. *Epistle* LVIII.2 in *The Treatises of S. Caecilius Cuyprian* 144.

37. *Epistle* LVIII.11, in *The Treatises of S. Caecilius Cyprian* 149.

38. This is Hermas' third vision. In William Jardine, adapted and intro., *Shepherd of Hermas: The Gentle Apocalypse*, (Redwood City, CA: Proteus, 1992) 35-36, ch. 4, 5.

In the *Martyrdom of Marian and James*, Marian sees Cyprian "at the judge's right hand." Musurillo 203, ch. 6.10. In addition, in the "Last Judgement," martyrs stand with God in judging others. See for example, Origen's *An Exhortation to Martyrdom* XXVIII, in Rowan A. Greer, trans. and intro., *Origen: An Exhortation to Martyrdom, Prayer, First Principles: Book IV, Prologue to the Commentary on the Song of Songs, Homily XXVII on Numbers* (New York: Paulist, 1979) 60; Tertulllian's *Ad Martyras* ch.II; Rev. 21:8; Frend 91.

39. The notion of attaining God's favor also seems to be linked to the belief that martyrs were thought to have been selected from before time. In the Martyrdom of Fructuosus and Companions, for example (in the manuscript cited by F. Cavalieri, part of which is included in Musurillo) bishop Fructuosus appears to various Christians and says "all of these [i.e. the martyrs] God the Father, with God the Son and the Holy Spirit, chose within himself before the world was made" (185, n. 15).

40. See, for example, the *Martyrs of Lyons* in Musurillo 77, chs. 45-46 and 85, chs. 6-8. See also Origen's *An Exhortation to Martyrdom*, especially chs. XXXVII, XXXVIII and XLIX in Greer 68-70, 77-79 and ch. 2 of this book.

41. Musurillo 183, ch. 6. 1.

42. Musurillo 183, ch. 6.2. Note, in the manuscripts cited by Cavalieri, that bishop Fructuosus appeared to Christians who had gathered the ashes and reprimanded them for ignoring the rest of the church by keeping the ashes to themselves. He then instructed them to "gather all of our remains...together," so that "all of you and your children" could "make supplication together and praise God...." Here, the exhortation is against having acted selfishly and not against gathering the ashes. The ashes were immediately brought to the church and buried under the altar (Musurillo 185, n. 15). In the adapted version used by Musurillo (from P. Franchi de' Cavalieri) the bishop simply "urged them [i.e. the

parishioners] that what each had taken of his ashes out of love for him should be restored without delay" (186, ch. 6).

43. Musurillo 111, ch. 4.1.
44. Musurillo 111, ch. 4.1.
45. Musurillo 111, ch. 4.2.
46. Musurillo 111, ch. 4.2.
47. Musurillo 111, ch. 4.2.
48. Musurillo 117, ch. 7.10.
49. Musurillo 125, ch. 17.2.
50. Musurillo 125, ch. 17.2.
51. Musurillo 125, ch. 16.3.
52. Musurillo 125, ch. 16.4.
53. Musurillo 127, ch. 18.4.
54. Musurillo 127, ch. 18.5.
55. The martyrdom was on the anniversary of Geta's birthday and would have drawn a large crowd. Musurillo 125, n. 15. See also Banes, "Pre-Decian *Acta Martyrum*" 522-3.
56. Musurillo 129, ch. 20.
57. Musurillo 129, ch. 20.10.
58. (Ithaca, NY: Cornell UP, 1991) 19.
59. Atkinson 19.
60. Atkinson 19.
61. Atkinson 19. See also 20-22.
62. Musurillo 75, ch. 41.
63. In support, see Patricia Cox Miller, "'A Dubious Twilight': Reflections on Dreams in Patristic Literature," *Church History* 55 (1986):160.

# Concluding Essay

The importance of visions for the early church is attested to throughout its scriptures and early church documents.[1] This importance was enhanced further through the church's experience of persecution, resulting in the delineation and appropriation of the martyrs' visions as prophetic epiphanies meant to exhort, console and strengthen the church as a whole. The prophetic nature of the martyrs' visions--as interpreted by the community's ownership of them-- further emphasized the importance of the *content* of the visions and the martyr's interpretation (when given).

Analysis of the visions of, for example, Perpetua, Saturus, Polycarp, and others studied within this book, shows that this content could, and often was, interpreted subversively. Through the visions, the grandeur and power of the Roman state, for example, could become subverted by glimpses of the kin-dom of God, and the primacy given to earthly life (thus the Roman use of the threat of death to coerce Christians into submission) was upstaged by interstitial experiences of eternal glory. Further, when the content was considered in relation to the seer's status and gender, it created a strong propensity for interpretations that defied theological and ecclesiastical norms. Popular (theological) beliefs regarding the martyr's mediatorial abilities and eschatological privileges were among these.

Popular views about martyrs, as well as the martyrs' experience of being a community that was set apart and unique, worked synergistically challenging established ecclesiastical borders by casting women and non-ordained men in priestly roles. Women such as Perpetua could function in ways that defied common practice regarding women's roles in the church, and in society. Perpetua's function as mediator on behalf of her deceased brother Dinocrates developed to include advocacy to, and pastoral ministry for, her fellow martyrs. Amidst her new *comunitas* of martyrs, her mediatorial functions were not only accepted, but valued as God-given gifts that benefited all. However, ecclesiastical efforts to curtail the mediatorial authority ascribed to the members of the *comunitas*, the end of persecution, and the ecclesiastical and cultural impact of the absorption of the church into the Roman empire through Constantine, would make this experience short-lived.

The study of these visions has also proved fruitful in other ways. Through Saturus' vision one is able to get a better appreciation for the historical and theological issues that were besetting him and his community. A strong dispensational belief, for instance, explains why Saturus' vision of paradise did not contain the tree of life, nor the river of life that, as portrayed in the book of Revelation, flowed from the throne of God. Further, the emphatic allusions to the Hebrew Temple in light of New Covenant theology--that focused on the God-Christ seated at the throne where gentiles were touched and made anew-- reflects, among other, Christianity's need to assert itself over its religious and politically favored rival, Judaism. The ongoing animosity that divided the (e.g. Carthaginian) Jews and the Christians, the Old Covenant from the New, is also evident throughout some of the Acts and other early church documents.

Finally, a study of the visions of the various martyrs included in this study has helped to underline the importance that documents, many of which were not included in the church canon (not excluding other pagan texts), exercised upon the ideas and beliefs of early church Christians.

# Appendix A

## Textual Studies on the Martyrdom of Perpetua and Felicitas

These textual studies include the following: C. J. M. J. van Beek, *Passio sanctarum Perpetuae et Felicitatis* (Nijmegen, 1936)1-62; Rendel J. Harris and Seth K. Gifford, eds., *The Acts of Martyrdom of Perpetua and Felicitas: The original Greek text now first edited from a ms. in the library of the Convent of the Holy Sepulcher at Jerusalem* (London: Clay, 1890), includes the longer and shorter Latin texts as well as the Greek text; Giuseppi Lazzati, 'Note critiche al testo della "Passio SS. Perpetuae et Felicitatis,"' *Aevum* 30 (1956), 30-5, with the critical apparatus in *Gli suiluppi della letteratura sui martiri nei primi quattro secoli* (Società editrice internazionale, Turin, 1956)177-89; Herbert Anthony Musurillo, intro. and trans., *The Acts of the Christian Martyrs* (Oxford, Clarendon, 1972); Armitage J. Robinson, ed. *"The Passion of S. Perpetua:" Texts and Studies* 1:2 (Cambridge: The UP, 1891 as reprinted in Nedelm: Kraus Reprint Limited, 1967), includes the longer and shorter Latin texts and the Greek text; W. H. Shewring, *The Passion of SS. Perpetua and Felicity: A New Edition and Translation of the Latin Text Together with the Sermons of S. Augustine Upon These Saints* (London: Sheed,1931), contains the longer Latin text; R. E. Wallis, "The Martyrdom of Perpetua and Felicitas," eds. Alexander Roberts and James Donaldson in *Ante-Nicene Fathers* (Grand Rapids: Eerdmans, 1973) 3: 699-706.

On establishing the date of the *passio* see T. D. Barnes, "Pre-Decian *Acta Martyrum,*" *Journal of Theological Studies* 19 (1968): 52

# Appendix B

## Review of the Related Literature

At the time of this study, I found no studies that dealt specifically *with the subversive dimensions of the visions of the martyrs of the second to fourth centuries*. The only work that I discovered that indirectly deals with the topic of vision and martyrdom is the book by Cecil M. Robeck, Jr., *Prophecy in Carthage: Perpetua, Tertullian, and Cyprian* (Cleveland: Pilgrim, 1992). Robeck's focus on prophetic gifts necessarily involves the experience of visions. However, this involvement is limited to discussing the factors that gave rise to prophetic gifts in Carthage--as evinced within the *Martyrdom of Perpetua and Felicitas* and the writings of Tertullian and Cyprian. He concludes that Persecution and the New Prophecy (i.e. Montanism) gave cause for the experience of prophetic gifts in Carthage. My book on the visions of the martyrs adds to this work by delving into the content of second to fourth century visions and exploring how these may have functioned within their contexts. Though not its primary intention, this study will also show that the widespread experience of visions among martyrs beyond Carthage, and the early church view that martyrs were especially blessed with visions, may have had less to do with the influence of the New Prophecy and more to do with the Hebrew and Christian tradition about the martyr as prophet. Another book that relates to my topic but does not encompass it is William C. Weinrich's book, *Spirit and Martyrdom: A Study of the Work of the Holy Spirit in Contexts of Persecution and Martyrdom in the New Testament and Early Christian Literature* (Washington: UP of America, 1981). This book is primarily concerned with the spiritual nature of Christian martyrdom. The section on the visions of Perpetua, for example, concentrates on showing how, by the third century, christological and ecclesiological views of martyrdom begin to be supplanted by an ethical perspective.

Patricia Cox Miller's creative and insightful, *Dreams in Late Antiquity: Studies in the Imagination of a Culture* (Princeton: Princeton UP, 1994) is more broad based and theoretical. In particular she looks at the classificatory systems and significance of dreams for pagans, Jews and Christians in the second to the fifth centuries. Cox Miller argues that dreams played an important emotional and discursive role in the ethical and philosophical realms of Graeco-Roman dreamers. She further proposes that the study of dream literature provides an important venue to a better understanding of late antique culture. My study contributes to Cox Miller's by affirming the intricate role visions played, especially in the life of the martyr and the persecuted church (often times, martyrs referred to their dreams as visions). The communal ownership of the martyrs' visions (I argue this in ch. 2), for example, directly supports the early church's view of visions as valuable to their emotional and spiritual life (see especially chs. 3 and 4).

However, this aspect of the communal ownership of the visions of the martyrs makes them unique. Unlike the dreams of, for instance, Jerome or Aelius Aristides, which Cox Miller explores, the visions of the martyrs not only carried divine authority, they were also considered prophetic--their message was meant to address (e.g. exhort, console, admonish) Christians of all times and places. This criterion had a lasting theological and historical effect upon Christians, not the least of which can be seen in later sermons about these visions and the cult of the martyrs. Thus, the context of persecution and the criterion of communal ownership leads me toward a different argument. Where Cox Miller argues that individual Graeco-Roman dreamers used dreams to construct worlds of personal meaning, I would have to argue that this meaning was already present in their decision to die for their faith, and that visions served to enhance and further elucidate this meaning. Finally, unlike Cox Miller, I do not enter into psychological analyses of the visions/dreams. Her study of Perpetua's visions, for example, focuses on them as *oneiric* experiences—"as expressions of transformations of self-identity and deepened self-consciousness."[30] My focus is primarily on the seer and/or community's interpretation or possible interpretation of the vision and how this informs us.

An article that approximates my topic of subversion is the short, but interesting article by Rebecca Lyman, "Perpetua: A Christian Quest for Self." In her article Lyman uses the visions along with Perpetua's reflections on her family "to look at the interior development of Perpetua herself in relation to her social context and spiritual experience as recorded in her diary."[31] Her conclusion emphasizes Perpetua's use of her freedom of choice to challenge given definitions about women and their interior life. Her work offers important new insights to women's studies and locates and addresses subversive dimensions within this *passio*. My study adds to this argument in a unique way. It will show that the martyrdom of Perpetua is not only about her interior development but about her leadership and priestly development. Further, it will show that within the community of martytrs, this development was not only valued, but encouraged (see especially ch. 6).

One other work that deserves mention is Violet MacDermot's, The Cult of the Seer in the Ancient Middle East: A contribution to Current Research on Hallucinations Drawn from Coptic and Other Texts (Berkeley: U of California

P, 1971). This book looks at the lives, the ascetic practices and the 'visions' of a group of seers (Egyptian, Greek, Jewish) of the early Christian period. The collection of visions contained are juxtaposed thematically (not chronologically) and the relationship and development of those themes, along with its medical-social value, are considered. I have found MacDermot's inter-textual and historical analyses of the themes inherent in the different visions valuable. Nevertheless, the aim and purpose of her book are different in scope. Her work is a contribution to the "disturbing feature of modern literature on hallucinations and hallucinogenic techniques..." and its "tendency to assume that experiences achieved by such methods as drug-taking are comparable or even identical with those of the seers of ancient religious history."[32] Her work, therefore, is medical-historical and the aim is to "distinguish the visions of the seers from the modern 'psychedelic' experiences."[33]

The above literary evidence revealed, at the time, a historical/theological lacuna in this area of scholarship that needed to be bridged. Thus, the intent of this study.

## Literary and Historical Studies

Since Ruinart's first monumental collection of the *Acts*, there have been many and varied attempts at determining historicity. Because the veracity of my study does not depend on the "authenticity" of the *Passiones* (or Martyrdoms contained within the Acts) but aims at determining whether these may have contained any subversive elements, I will limit myself here to citing the most important and influential of the literary/historical studies. For further information I refer the reader to Musurillo's book, *The Acts of the Christian Martyrs* which contains a section on "Tradition and Form in the Acts of the Christian Martyrs" (l-lii).

Although it was Edmond Le Blant[34] who first attempted to determine the authenticity through the use of "form" analysis, it was the Bollandiste Hippolyte Delehaye[35] whose comparative analysis provided some sense of literary and historical parameters for distinguishing between the nature and function of these *actas*.[36] While Delehaye's six distinctions are "sound as far as they go," according to Musurillo "the question of ultimate historicity, or how far our documents reflect the actual events of the period of persecution, leaves the scholar in an embarrassing dilemma."[37] Apart from the evidence of Eusebius, scholars are without external confirmation of the facts and made to rely on "those texts which seem least objectionable from the historical point of view." It is for this reason, Musurillo admits, that the acceptance of the *Acts*, especially those in his present collection, "remains a provisory and tentative one." Further, he alludes to the genre of the Acts as that of "Christian witness" making the separation of the "factual record (*hypomnema*) from *apologia* and *didache*" difficult. He thus concludes that because of this, it is "unreasonable to suppose that any general norms can be defined that would apply to all of these Acts."[38]

## Sources of Extant Acts

Our extant Acts come from varied sources. Included among these are official church collections, most important of which is Eusebius of Caesarea's *Ecclesiastical History*. (His book, for example, is the only source for the text of the *Letter of the Churches of Lyons and Vienne* where we are told of the brutal uprising in Gaul and the ensuing martyrdom of many Christians there.) His collection, *On the Ancient Martyrs*, now lost, is known through the repeated references made to it in his *EH*. From North Africa we have the *Martyrdom of Perpetua and Felicitas*, the *Acts of Cyprian*, the *Martyrdom of Marian and James* and the *Martyrdom of Montanus and Lucius*. Musurillo points out that this cluster of African Latin *acta matyrum*, as well as the *Passio Crispinae* and the *Martyrdom of Fructuosus and Companions*, "was beloved by St. Augustine and his community at Hippo."[39]

From Panonia in the first quarter of the fourth century there emanated yet another group of Acts.[40] Of these we have only the *Passio Irenaei* and the *Passio Pollionis*.

The monumental task of collecting and compiling the Acts was undertaken first by the Bollandists and, then by Thierry Ruinart.[41] Since then, the *Acts* have been the subject of numerous critical studies.[42] These studies are currently available in a variety of modern languages and within such academically diverse fields as sociology and psychoanalysis. My excursion into the Acts, however, will take another direction.

# Bibliography

## On Martyrdom
## (and Martyrological Hagiographical Literature)

Allard, Paul. *Ten Lectures on the Martyrs*. Trans. Juigi Cappadelta. New York: Benziger, 1907.

Amore, A. "Persecuzioni." *Enciclopedia cattolica*. (1952) 9: 1198-1202.

Armitage, Bedjan, P., ed. *Acta Martyrum et Sanctorum, I-VII*. Paris, 1890-97.

Attwater, Donald. *Martyrs, from St. Stephen to John Tung*. New York: Sheed, 1957.

Bisbee, Gary A. *Pre-Decian Acts of Martyrs and Commentarii*. Philadelphia: Fortress, 1988.

Delehaye, H. "Cinq Leçons sur la Méthode Hagiographique." *Subsidia Hagiographica* 21
Brussels: Société des Bollandistes, 1934.

_____. "Les Origines du Culte des Martyrs." *Subsidia Hagiographica* 20 2$^e$ ed. Brussels: Société des Bollandietes, 1933.

_____. "Les Passions des Martyrs et les Genres Littéraires." *Subsidia Hagiographica*. 13b. 2$^e$ ed. Brussels: Société des Bollandiestes, 1966.

_____. "Sanctus. Essai sur le Culte des Saints dans l'Antiquité." *Subsidia Hagiographica*. Brussels: Société des Bollandistes, 1927.

Dodds, E. R. *Pagan and Christian in an Age of Anxiety*. Cambridge: UP, 1965.

Droge, Arthur J. and James D. Tabor. *A Noble Death: Suicide & Martyrdom Among Christians and Jews in Antiquity*. New York: Harper, 1992.

Formby, Henry. *The Little Book of the Martyrs of the City of Rome*. London: Burns, 1877.

Friedh, Åke. "Le Probleme de la Passion des Saintes Perpétue et Félicité." *Studia Græca et Latina Gothoburgensia*. Vol. 26. Goteborg: Almquist, 1968.

Harnack, Adolph. "Persecution of Christians." *Schaff-Herzog Encyclopedia of Religious Knowledge*. (1910) 8: 467-9.

Holl, Karl. "Gesammelte Aufsatze zur Kirchengeschichte." *Der Osten* (Tübingen: Mohr, 1928) 2: 68-102.

Hummel, Edelhard Leonhard. *The Concept of Martyrdom According to St. Cyprian of Carthage*. Washington, DC: Catholic U of America P, 1946.

Ide, Arthur Frederick and Charles Anthony Stanley Ide. *Woman in the Age of Christian Martyrs*. Mesquite: Ide, 1980.

Klawiter, Frederick C. "The Role of Martyrdom and Persecution in Developing the Priestly Authority of Women in Early Christianity: A Case Study of Montanism." *Church History* 49 (1980): 251-261.

Knopf, R. *Ausgewählte Märtyrerakten*. Tübingen and Leipzig, 1901; 3$^d$ ed. G. Krüger, 1929; 4$^{th}$ ed. G. Ruhbach, 1965.

Lefkowitz, Mary R. "Motivations for St. Perpetua's Martyrdom." *Journal of the American Academy of Religion*. 44 (1976): 417-421.

Lods, Marc. "Confesseurs et Martyrs: Successeurs des Prophetes dans l'Eglise des Trois Premiers Siécles". *Cahiers Théologiques*. Vol. 41. Neuchatel: Delachaux, 1958.

Mason, Arthur James. *The Historic Martyrs of the Primitive Church*. New York, 1905.

O'Meara, John. Commentary. *Prayer: Exhortation to Martyrdom*. Origen. Trans. O'Meara. Westminster, MD: Newman, 1954.

Rahner, Carl. *Visions and Prophecies*. New York: Herder, 1963.

Riddle, Donald Wayne. *The Martyrs: A Study in Social Control*. Chicago: U of Chicago P, 1931.

Robinson, Armitage J., ed. "The Passion of S. Perpetua." *Texts and Studies* 1(2). Cambridge: Cambridge UP, 1891.

Rossi, Mary Ann. "The Passion of Perpetua, Every Woman of Late Antiquity." *Pagan and Christian Anxiety: A Response to E. R. Dodds*. Ed. R. Smith and J. Lounibos. Lanham, MD: UP of America, 1984.

Russo-Alesi and Anthony Ignatius, eds. *Martyrology Pronouncing Dictionary*. New York: O'Toole, 1939.

Seeley, David. "The Noble Death: Greco-Roman Martyrology and Paul's Concept of Salvation."
*Journal for the Study of the New Testament Supplement Series*. n. 28. Sheffield, 1990.

Sherwin-White, A. N. "The Early Persecutions and Roman Law Again." *Journal of Theological Studies* 3 (1952): 199-213.

Weinrich, William C. *Spirit and Martyrdom: A Study of the Work of the Holy Spirit in Contexts of Persecution and Martyrdom in the New Testament and Early Christian Literature*. Washington, D.C.: UP of America, 1981.

Williams, Sam K. "Jesus' Death as Saving Event: The Background and Origin of a Concept." *Harvard Dissertations in Religion*. Missoula, MT: Scholars, 1975.

Workman, Herbert B. *The Martyrs of the Early Church*. London: Kelly, 1913.

Zeiller, Jacques. "Legalité et Arbittraire dans les Persécutions Contre les Chrétiens." *Analecta Bollandiana*. Paris, 1882.

# On Martyrdom and Visions

Dronke, Peter. *Women Writers of the Middle Ages: A Critical Study of Texts from Perpetua (†203) to*

*Marguerite Porete (†1310)*. Cambridge: Cambridge UP, 1984.
Fischel, H. A. "Martyr and Prophet: A Study in Jewish Literature." *Jewish Quarterly Review* (1946/7): 364-370.
James, M. R., ed. "Martyrdom of St. Paul." *The Apocryphal New Testament*. 1924.
\_\_\_\_. "Martyrdom of St. Peter." *The Apocryphal New Testament*. 1924.
Mac Dermot, Violet. *The Cult of the Seer in the Ancient Middle East: A Contribution to Current Research on Hallucinations Drawn from Coptic and Other Texts*. Berkeley, U of California P, 1971.
Meslin, Michel. "Vases Sacres et Boissons d'Ternit dans les Visions des Martyrs Africains." *Epektasis:Melanges Patristiques*. Ed. J. Fonaine, 1972, 139-153.
Miller Cox, Patricia. *Dreams in Late Antiquity: Studies in the Imagination of Culture*. Princeton: Princeton UP, 1994.
Petraglio, R. "Des Influences de l'Apocalypse dans le 'Passio Perpetuae'." *L'Apocalypse de Jean: Traditions Exégétiques et Iconographiques IIIe-XIIIe Siécles*. Genéve: Droz, 1979.
Roebeck, Cecil M. Jr. *Prophecy in Carthage:Perpetua, Tertullian, and Cyprian*. Cleveland: Pilgram, 1992.
Turin, Domenico Devoti. "La Passion de Perpétue: Un Noeud Familial." *Studia Patristica* Ed. Elizabeth A. Livingstone. Leuven: Peeters, 1989.

## Historical background

Atkinson, Clarissa W. *The Oldest Vocation: Christian Motherhood in the Middle Ages*. London: Cornell UP, 1991.
Aune, David E. *Prophecy in Early Christianity and the Ancient Mediterranean World*. Grand Rapids, MI: Eerdmans, 1983.
Babut, E. "L' Adoration des Empereurs et l'Origine de la Persécution de Dioclétien." *Revue Historique* 123 (1916): 222.
van Beek, Cornelis I. M. I. *"Passio Sanctarum Perpetuae et Felicitatis." Florilegium Patristicum*, 43. Bonn: Hanstein, 1938.
Baynes, Norman H. "The Great Persecution." *Cambridge Ancient History* vol. 12. London: Cambridge UP, 1970-1992.
Buschholz, Dennis D. *Your Eyes Will Be Opened: A Study of the Greek (Ethiopic) Apocalypse of Peter*. Atlanta: Scholars, 1988.
Charles, R. H. *Eschatology: The Doctrine of a Future Life in Israel, Judaism, and Christianity, A Critical History*. 1913. New York: Schocken, 1963.
Cody, Aelred. *Heavenly Sanctuary and Liturgy in the Epistle to the Hebrews: The Achievement of Salvation in the Epistle's Perpectives*. St. Meinrad, IN: Grail, 1960.
Collins, John J. "Apocalyptic Eschatology as the Transcendence of Death." *Catholic Biblical Quarterly* 36 (1974): 21-43.
Danielou, Jean. *The Angels and Their Mission*.Trans. David Heiman. Maryland: Newman, 1957.

Daube, David. "Death as a Release in the Bible." *Novum Testamentum* 5 (1962): 82-104.

Deshaies, Bariel. *Studies in Ancient Society*, M. I. Finley, ed. *Past and Present*. London: Routledge, 1974.

Dodd, C. H. *The Interpretation of the Fourth Gospel*. Cambridge: Cambridge UP, 1953.

Dunnil, John. *Covenant and Sacrifice in the Letter to the Hebrews*. Cambridge: Cambridge UP, 1992.

Fox, Lane Robin. *Pagans and Christians*. New York: Knopf, 1987.

Frend, W. H. C. *Martyrdom and Persecution in the Early Church: A Study of a Conflict from the Maccabees to Donatus*. 1965. Garden City, NY: Anchor, 1967.

———. "Two Notes on the Great Persecution," *Studies in Church History* 2 (1965).

Gager, John G. "Religion and Social Class in the Early Roman Empire." Eds. S. Benko and J. H.

O' Rourke. *The Catacombs and the Colosseum: The Roman Empire as the Setting of Primitive Christianity*. Valley Forge: Judson, 1971.

González, Justo L. *The Story of Christianity*. 2 vols. San Francisco: Harper, 1984.

Grant, Michael. *The Climax of Rome: The Final Achievements of the Ancient World A.D. 161-337*. New York: New American Library, 1968.

Gregg, J. A. *The Decian Persecution*. London, n.p., 1897.

Hamman, André. *Baptism: Ancient Liturgies and Patristic Texts*. New York: Alba, 1967.

Jardine, William, Introduction. *Shepherd of Hermas: The Gentle Apocalypse: A Vision of Millennial Hope From Ancient Christianity*. Redwood City, CA: Proteus, 1992.

Lawlor, Hugh Jackson and John E. L. Oulton. Introduction and notes. *Eusebius, Bishop of Caesarea, The Ecclesiastical History and Martyrs of Palestine*. Eusebius. 2 vols. Trans. Lawlor and Oulton. 1928. London: Society for Promoting Christian Knowledge, 1954.

Leclercq, Dom H. *L'afrique Chrétienne*. 2 vols. Paris: Librairie Victor Lecoffre, 1904.

Lindars, Barnabas. *The Theology of the Letter to the Hebrews*. Cambridge: Cambridge UP, 1991.

Maraval, Pierre. *Les Persecutions Durant les Quatre Premiers Siecles du Christianism*. Paris: Desclee, 1992.

Meeks, Wayne. "The Image of Androgyne: Some Uses of a Symbol in Earliest Christianity." *History of Religions* 13 (1974): 165-208.

Melmoth, William. Introduction. *Epistolae*. Pliny. Trans. Melmoth. Critical ed., E. G. Hardy. Oxford, 1889.

Members of the English Church, Introduction. *Treatises of S. Caecilius Cyprian Bishop of Carthage, and Martyr*. Oxford: Parker, 1876.

Monceaux, Paul. *Histoire Littéraire de l'Afrique Chrétienne Depuis les Origines Jusqu'a l'Invasion Arabe*. 7 vols. Paris: Leroux, 1901-1905.

Palmer, D. W. "To Die Is Gain' (Philippians i 21)."*Novum Testamentum* 17 (1975): 203-18.
Quasten, Johannes. *Patrology.* 3 vols. Utrecht-Antwerp: Spectrum, 1975.
Rahner, Karl. *Visions and Prophecies.* Freiburg: Herder, 1963.
Ricciotti, Giuseppe. *The Age of Martyrs: Christianity from Diocletian to Constantine.* Trans. Anthony Bull. Milwaukee: Bruce, 1959.
Richardson, Cyril C., Translation. *Early Christian Fathers.* Ed., Richardson. New York: Macmillan, 1970.
Rowland, Christopher. *The Open Heaven: A Study of Apocalyptic in Judaism and Early Christianity.* New York: Crossroad, 1982.
Rowley, H. H. *Worship in Ancient Israel: Its Forms and Meaning.* Philadelphia: Fortress, 1962.
Ruffin, Bernard. *The Days of the Martyrs: A History of the Persecution of Christians from Apostolic Times to the Time of Constantine.* Huntington, IN: Our Sunday Visitor, 1985. de Ste Croix, G. E. M. "Aspects of the 'Great' Persecution.'" *Harvard Theological Review* 47 (1954): 75-113.
Salisbury, F. S. and H. Mattingly. "The Reign of Trajan Decius." *Journal of Roman Studies* 14 (1924): 1-23.
Saxer, Victor. "Afrique Latine." *Hagiographies: International History of the Latin and Vernacular Hagiographical Literature in the West from its Origins to 1550.* In *Corpus Christianorum.* Brepols, 1994.
Schaff, Phillip. *History of the Christian Church: Ante-Nicene Christianity.* 8 vols. 1887. Grand Rapids: Eerdmans, 1970.
Sherman, J. Edward. *The Nature of Martyrdom: A Dogmatic and Moral Analysis According to the Teaching of St. Thomas Aquinas.* Paterson, NJ: St. Anthony, 1942.
_____. *The Roman Citizenship.* 2nd ed. Oxford: Clarendon, 1973.
Soltau, Henry W. *The Holy Vessels and Furniture of the Tabernacle.* Grand Rapids, MI: Kregel, 1969.
Steinhauser, Kenneth. "Augustine's Reading of the *Passio sanctarum Perpetuae et Felicitatis.*"
*Studia Patristica.* Ed. Elizabeth A. Livingstone. Leuven: Peeters, 1997.
Volken, Laurent. *Visions, Revelations and the Church.* Trans., Edward Gallagher. New York: Kennedy, 1963.
Wescott, Brooke Foss. *Epistle to the Hebrews: The Greek Text with Notes and Essays.* London: Macmillan, 1928.
Whitaker, E. C. *Documents of the Baptismal Liturgy.* London: S. P. C. K., 1970.

## Reference: Semiotics

Clarke, D. S., Jr. *Principles of Semiotic.* New York: Routledge, 1987.
Deeley, John. *Basics of Semiotics.* Indianapolis: Indiana University Press, 1990.
Eco, Umberto. *A Theory of Semiotics.* Bloomington: Indiana UP, 1976.

García-Rivera, Alex. *St. Martín de Porres: The "Little Stories and the Semiotics of Culture*. Maryknoll, New York: Orbis, 1995.

Graves, R. *Greek Myths.* 2 Vols. n.p.: Penguin, 1955.

Merrell, Floyd. *Semiotic Foundations: Steps Toward an Epistemology of Written Texts*. Bloomington, IN: UP, 1982.

Noth, Winfried. *Handbook of Semiotics*. Bloomington, IN: Indiana UP, 1990.

Stock, Brian. *Listening for the Text: On the Uses of the Past*. Baltimore: Hopkins UP, 1990.

## Reference: General

Abbott-Smith, G. *A Manual Greek Lexicon of the New Testament*. 3rd ed. Edinburgh: Clark, 1964.

Andrews, E. A., ed. *Harpers' Latin Dictionary: A New Latin Dictionary*. Rev. and enlarged ed. Charlton T. Lewis and Charles Short. New York: American, 1907.

Alter, Robert and Frank Kermode, eds. *The Literary Guide to the Bible*. Cambridge: Harvard UP, 1987.

Artemidorus, Daldianus. *The Interpretation of Dreams: Oneirocritica*. Trans. and Comment., Robert J. White. Park Ridge, NJ: Noyes, 1975.

Bhabha, Homi K. *The Location of Culture*. New York: Routledge, 1994.

Boardman, John, Jasper Griffin and Oswyn Murray. *The Oxford History of the Classical World*. New York: Oxford, 1986.

Draisma, Sipke, ed. *Intertextuality in Biblical Writings: Essays in Honour of Bas van Iersel*. Kampen: Uitgeversmaatschappij J. H. Kok, 1989.

Farbridge, Maurice H. *Studies in Biblical and Semitic Symbolism*. New York, KTAV, 1970.

Gingrich, Wilbur F. and Frederick W. Danker. *A Greek-English Lexicon of the New Testament and Other Early Christian Literature*. Walter Bauer, ed. 2nd ed. Trans. and adapt. William F. Arndt and F. Wilbur Gingrich. Chicago: UP of Chicago, 1979.

Isasi-Díaz, María and Yolanda Tarango. *Hispanic Women: Prophetic Voice in the Church*. San Francisco: Harper, 1988.

Keen, Sam. *Voices and Visions*. New York: Harper, 1974.

Lampe, G. W. H., ed. *A Patristic Greek Lexicon*. Oxford: Clarendon, 1961.

Migne, J. P., ed. *Patrilogiae Graecae*. 168 vols.Rpt. Tumholti, Belg.: Typographi Brepols, 1978.

Rahner, Karl. *On the Theology of Death*. Trans. Charles H. Henkey. New York: Herder, 1961.

www.ingramcontent.com/pod-product-compliance
Lightning Source LLC
Chambersburg PA
CBHW052212240426
43670CB00036B/194